BIG QUESTIONS

Developing a Christ-Centered Apologetic

Andy McLean

© 2016 Lifeway Press®
Reprinted Aug. 2017, Nov. 2017, June 2018, July 2020, Sept. 2020, Dec. 2020, June 2021

ISBN: 9781430041542
Item: 005737732

Dewey decimal classification: 239
Subject headings: RELIGION / CHRISTIAN MINISTRY / YOUTH

To order additional copies of this resource, write to Lifeway Resources Customer
Service; One Lifeway Plaza; Nashville, TN 37234-0113; fax 615.251.5933; phone toll free
800.458.2772; order online at *www.lifeway.com;* email *orderentry@lifeway.com;*
or visit the Lifeway Christian Store serving you.

Printed in the United States of America.
Student Ministry Publishing
Lifeway Resources
One Lifeway Plaza
Nashville, TN 37234-0144

CONTENTS

ABOUT THE AUTHOR

 ANDY MCLEAN serves as the editor for
The Gospel Project for Students at Lifeway Christian
Resources in Nashville, Tennessee. A life-long learner
in the areas of theology and apologetics, Andy has
earned a Bachelor of Arts (B.A.) in religion, a Master of
Divinity (MDiv) in apologetics from Southeastern Baptist
Theological Seminary, a Master of Arts (M.A.) in Science
and Religion from Biola University, a Master of Theology
(Th.M) in Philosophy of Religion from Southeastern Baptist
Theological Seminary, and is currently working toward a Ph.D in Systematic Theology
from the University of Aberdeen.

In addition to working in Christian publishing, Andy has been actively involved in
student ministry in various capacities over the past 15 years, whether it be on staff at
a church or teaching in the high school classroom. No matter the venue, it has always
been Andy's desire to not only help students develop a God-centered worldview, but
to also equip students to winsomely explain their worldview to others.

Andy and his wife, Sarah, have four children, Isaac, Caleb, Timothy, and Tobias.

HOW TO USE THIS RESOURCE

BEFORE THE SESSION

» Provide a book copy of *Big Questions* for each student.

» Set up a DVD player and cue the DVD to the correct session.

» Preview each session ahead of time, becoming familiar with both the layout and content of the leader guide located in the back of this book. The leader guide pages will contain not only the material supplied in the student pages, but additional (italicized) material that is unique and specific for the leader—such as potential answers to questions, illustrations, and additional content that will help you guide students through the group portion of the study.

THE SESSION

Each session is organized under the following headings:

START (5 – 10 minutes)

» This portion of the study provides an opening activity to begin each session.

WATCH (15 – 18 minutes)

» In this video portion of the group time, students will watch interviews with leading apologists, such as William Lane Craig, J. P. Moreland, Craig Hazen, and Sean McDowell.

» Each interview will cover one of the Big Questions addressed in the study.

» Students can follow along with each interview using the video guide. Answers to any fill-in-the-blanks can be found in the leader guide.

DISCUSS (35 – 40 minutes)

During group discussion you will...

» Discuss the interview.

» Review the video guide.

» Lead students through the questions, Scripture passages, and teaching material aimed at answering each Big Question. (For leaders, the same content found in the student pages can be found in the leader guide, with the addition of leader specific material in italics.)

DEVOTIONS (5 – 10 minutes of personal time each day)

The devotions provide additional material related to the topic for that session. Although they are intended for students, leaders are encouraged to read them as well. Each devotion will help provide clarity of understanding along with illustrations that help students connect the topic to everyday life.

WHAT DO I DO WITH MY DOUBTS?

START

SET THE SCENE

You and your best friend are studying together for an upcoming test. You notice that she isn't saying much—regarding school or anything else. You get a sense that something is troubling her, and after a little prompting she begins to explain how difficult life has been lately, especially when it comes to her faith in God. When you ask her what she means by that, she goes on to say that she's having all sorts of doubts about whether Christianity is true, whether the Bible is reliable, and whether Jesus is who He says He is, among other things. Not only that, but she starts to open up about some other difficulties in her home and social life, which makes you wonder what might be at the root of these struggles. Your friend looks directly at you with genuine sincerity and asks, "How can I know for sure my beliefs are true?" How do you respond?

WATCH

==≫

FROM THE INTERVIEW

Apologia – a verbal _____

Doubt is not necessarily a _____ thing.

Our answers to big questions _____ every decision that we make.

When people doubt, they tend to think it's only _____.

Identify the _____ of your doubts.

Doubt is not the _____ of faith.

Knowledge does not require _____.

Christianity is based upon claims to _____ _____.

IN YOUR OWN WORDS

Christian apologetics is about giving an intellectual defense of why we believe what we believe. Why do you think this is important?

How can apologetics not only help you defend your beliefs, but also encourage you in those beliefs?

How is apologetics ultimately about Jesus?

NOTES

In this section write down any additional thoughts, comments, or questions related to the interview.

DISCUSS

Have you ever experienced doubt when it comes to your beliefs? If so, what are some of the doubts or questions you've wrestled with?

How did having these doubts make you feel? Why do you think most people feel ashamed for having doubts or asking questions?

Did you share these doubts with a trusted friend? If so, what was the end result? If not, why?

What are the dangers of trying to think through our doubts alone?

How can avoiding the doubts we have hinder our ability to grow in our relationship with God?

In what ways could facing our doubts and seeking answers for them make us stronger Christians?

What do you think causes us to doubt? Why is it important to think about where our doubts stem from (intellectual, moral, volitional)?

FAITH AND DOUBT

What is faith? Here is a good working definition: "Faith is fundamentally a relational matter; it is about trusting God. Yet part of the inner dynamic of the life of faith is a desire to understand more about who and what we trust."[1] As Anselm said centuries ago, it is a faith that seeks understanding.

When it comes to faith, there are three important ways the Bible describes what it means in the life of a Christian:

Faith as:

Trust:

Understanding:

Obedience:

According to the Bible, faith has never been something that goes against reason. Instead, the Bible always presents faith as reasonable belief, founded upon evidences and historical events that took place in time-space-history. This is why Christian apologists throughout the centuries have defended their faith against critics by pointing out the intellectual and historical arguments that support the truthfulness of Christianity.

WHAT ARE SOME WAYS WE CAN GO ABOUT STRENGTHENING OUR FAITH?

1. LOOK TO SCRIPTURE.

Read Romans 4:18-21.

> He believed, hoping against hope, so that he became the father of many nations according to what had been spoken: So will your descendants be. He considered his own body to be already dead (since he was about 100 years old) and also considered the deadness of Sarah's womb, without weakening in the faith. He did not waver in unbelief at God's promise but was strengthened in his faith and gave glory to God, because he was fully convinced that what He had promised He was also able to perform.

How was Abraham strengthened in his own faith?

Why do you think this is God's primary means to strengthening one's faith?

2. LOOK TO JESUS.

Read Hebrews 12:1-2.

> Therefore, since we also have such a large cloud of witnesses surrounding us, let us lay aside every weight and the sin that so easily ensnares us. Let us run with endurance the race that lies before us, keeping our eyes on Jesus, the source and perfecter of our faith, who for the joy that lay before Him endured a cross and despised the shame and has sat down at the right hand of God's throne.

How do these verses describe Jesus' relationship to our faith?

Read John 1:45-46.

> Philip found Nathanael and told him, "We have found the One Moses wrote about in the Law (and so did the prophets): Jesus the son of Joseph, from Nazareth!" "Can anything good come out of Nazareth?" Nathanael asked him. "Come and see," Philip answered.

After having a personal encounter with Jesus, Philip couldn't help but point others to Him.

3. LOOK TO PEOPLE AROUND YOU.

Read Hebrews 13:7.

> Remember your leaders who have spoken God's word to you. As you carefully observe the outcome of their lives, imitate their faith.

Who are some biblical heroes in your own life that you can look to for answers when struggling with doubt?

TRUE STORY

As I mentioned in the video, my own story with doubt began in college and continued into my early years of seminary. For a long time it seemed and felt like I would always be plagued with questions in some form or another. Even when I would get some mental peace over a question I was struggling with, another one would inevitably pop up in its place. As a result, I felt like I was on this never-ending roller coaster, full of dramatic dips and corkscrews that were not only intellectual, but emotional as well given the overwhelming sense of shame I experienced during those seasons.

It was a difficult time in my life to say the least. However, I did eventually make it out of that place, in large part through the use of apologetics. The more I grew in my understanding of the Christian worldview, the better I became at discovering the reasons I believed what I believed. In doing so, I was able to address the questions that I struggled with.

I would be remiss not to tell you what took place during this time when I finally did open up to close friends about the questions I was wresting with. I initially struggled with the notion to "come clean" not only because of the shame I was feeling, but also because I didn't want to cause them to doubt as well. However, I was both amazed and somewhat relieved that many of my friends had been experiencing similar struggles. In fact, some of them were dealing with the exact questions that were troubling my own heart, but they felt ashamed to open up and share with others.

I say all of this to encourage you to not only meet your doubts and questions head-on with the truth of the Christian worldview, but also to encourage you to take up this approach alongside other Christian friends. By doing so, not only are you setting yourself up for your own success in this battle, but you could quite possibly be the encouragement someone else needs. Answers you've learned along your journey may play a crucial role in helping a friend in his or her own struggle with doubt.

WHEN DOUBTS BLOW OUR WAY

On that day, when evening had come, He told them, "Let's cross over to the other side of the sea." So they left the crowd and took Him along since He was already in the boat. And other boats were with Him. A fierce windstorm arose, and the waves were breaking over the boat, so that the boat was already being swamped. But He was in the stern, sleeping on the cushion. So they woke Him up and said to Him, "Teacher! Don't You care that we're going to die?"

He got up, rebuked the wind, and said to the sea, "Silence! Be still!" The wind ceased, and there was a great calm. Then He said to them, "Why are you fearful? Do you still have no faith?"

And they were terrified and asked one another, "Who then is this? Even the wind and the sea obey Him!"
—Mark 4:35-41

But let him ask in faith without doubting. For the doubter is like the surging sea, driven and tossed by the wind.

—Jas. 1:6

While surely not to the same degree, I know a little of what it is like to be stranded on a boat in the middle of open waters. In fact, just recently my wife and I took our oldest son out on what we thought would be a fishing adventure. I borrowed my brother's boat and by mid-morning we were at the boat launch ready to go. Things were pretty easy at first—we successfully got the boat into the water and everyone on board. After that, however, things began to get a little hectic.

For starters, it was blazing hot that day, and before we even left the dock we were feeling the effects of the heat. Second, because I wasn't familiar with my brother's new boat, I didn't know how to do certain things—key things like start the engine, for instance, or unlock the steering wheel. So there we were, having already pushed away from the dock, going adrift down the river unable to get the boat started. It wasn't too long before the wakes from other boats cast us to the sides of the banks and into the over-hanging trees and bushes (not a delightful place to be). We were completely helpless and at the mercy of the waves, being tossed around without any sense of control.

If you've ever struggled with doubts, then perhaps James' analogy resonates with you. Perhaps you feel as if your doubts are like a raging storm at sea, tossing you in every direction. Maybe you fear that this storm will never cease, but will eventually be your undoing. Perhaps you see yourself in a capsizing raft in a sea of confusion, wondering if rescue will ever be on its way.

If that's you, let me start off by encouraging you with one important truth: Look to Jesus! Sure, you have questions and doubts that need answers, questions perhaps about Jesus, other religions, or the existence of evil. However, as we begin to uncover answers to these questions, be encouraged from the outset to look to Jesus in your search for truth and hear what He has to say on the matter. Bring your doubts and fears to Him, share them with Him, and ask Him to open up your eyes to see how your questions might be answered. And when you approach the big questions in this way, your posture and mindset will be in a better position to learn and evaluate the answers you seek.

Have you ever felt tossed around as if on waves? How is doubt getting in the way of your faith today?

HEROES WHO SOMETIMES DOUBT (PART 1)

It's easy to fall into the mindset that Christians don't struggle with doubts about their beliefs. Not only that, but it's even easier to assume that strong Christians, those we see as being giants in the faith, don't struggle with doubts. Nothing could be further from the truth.

In Luke 7 we come across a scene where John the Baptist, imprisoned by Herod, begins to struggle with his faith in light of his circumstances. So much so that he sends some of his disciples to Jesus for confirmation that He is, in fact, who John imagined Him to be—the Messiah. Such a scene might seem odd to us at first, given that John was instrumental in the beginning stages of Jesus' ministry. It was John, if you recall, who first proclaimed that Jesus the Messiah had arrived, and it was John who publicly confessed that he himself was not worthy enough to even tie Jesus' sandals, much less baptize Him. However, despite having a strong start, John finds himself in a season of doubting, looking for personal assurance that his beliefs in Jesus are well-founded.

Even more remarkable than seeing a hero in the faith struggle with doubts like our own is Jesus' response. Some might imagine that Jesus, being discouraged by John's doubts, might use this as an opportunity to chide John for his lack of faith. But instead of telling John to "just have faith" or "just believe," Jesus graciously replies with reasons and evidences that, in the end, give assurance to John.

Jesus tells John the things that are taking place as a result of His ministry, such as the blind being able to see, the lame to walk, and the dead being raised to life. Of course, today readers might chalk that up to the fact that these signs and evidences are to encourage John in his faith because they were clearly supernatural works of God. And while that is certainly the case, it is also much more than that. The specific works Jesus was doing would have been reassuring to John not only because they are supernatural works of God, but also because they were fulfilling the Old Testament prophecies regarding the works of the Messiah who was to come. And by hearing that these things were taking place, Jesus was assuring John, through reasons and evidences, that his faith in Him was not at all a misplaced faith.

What does Jesus' response to John's struggle teach us about how God will respond when we doubt?

Then John's disciples told him about all these things. So John summoned two of his disciples and sent them to the Lord, asking, "Are You the One who is to come, or should we look for someone else?"

When the men reached Him, they said, "John the Baptist sent us to ask You, 'Are You the One who is to come, or should we look for someone else?'"

At that time Jesus healed many people of diseases, plagues, and evil spirits, and He granted sight to many blind people. He replied to them, "Go and report to John the things you have seen and heard: The blind receive their sight, the lame walk, those with skin diseases are healed, the deaf hear, the dead are raised, and the poor are told the good news. And anyone who is not offended because of Me is blessed."

—Luke 7:18-23

HEROES WHO SOMETIMES DOUBT (PART 2)

But one of the Twelve, Thomas (called "Twin"), was not with them when Jesus came. So the other disciples kept telling him, "We have seen the Lord!"

But he said to them, "If I don't see the mark of the nails in His hands, put my finger into the mark of the nails, and put my hand into His side, I will never believe!"

After eight days His disciples were indoors again, and Thomas was with them. Even though the doors were locked, Jesus came and stood among them. He said, "Peace to you!"

Then He said to Thomas, "Put your finger here and observe My hands. Reach out your hand and put it into My side. Don't be an unbeliever, but a believer."

Thomas responded to Him, "My Lord and my God!"

Jesus said, "Because you have seen Me, you have believed. Those who believe without seeing are blessed."
—John 20:24-29

Have you ever heard the phrase "doubting Thomas"? It's often used in reference to the disciple who wouldn't believe Jesus had been resurrected until he witnessed the risen Christ for himself. At other times the description is used in an uncomplimentary sense, labeling someone who doesn't believe what's being said as a "doubting Thomas."

It's unfortunate that Thomas is remembered not for some of the good things he said and did in the Gospels, but as the doubting disciple. (It was only a few chapters before this that we see Thomas display outstanding courage and willingness to be a martyr alongside Jesus.) However, maybe a little explanation will help put Thomas and his search for assurance in Jesus' resurrection in proper perspective.

It is important to remember that, as John stated, Thomas was not present when Jesus first appeared to the other disciples. Like ourselves, he didn't get the opportunity to be present when Jesus returned to show them His victory over sin and death. Thomas didn't get to witness with his own eyes and with his own hands the bodily resurrection of Jesus like his peers had. But did he really need to?

There's nothing wrong with wanting to see the evidence and reasons for your faith. Thomas was not necessarily in the wrong for wanting to see the tangible evidence for Jesus' resurrection. We know this because, at the very least, Jesus doesn't correct Thomas on this point. However, what we do see is that even apart from seeing firsthand the resurrection of Christ, Thomas still had ample reason to believe it was true. After all, he had been with Jesus for the previous three years of His ministry, witnessing what Jesus had done and even hearing Jesus speak of the fact that He would, eventually, be put to death yet rise again. Not only that, but Thomas was close to the other disciples who reported to him that Jesus had returned. He lived with them, served with them, shared countless meals with them, and knew the type of men they were and the character they possessed. All of these reasons, and many more, should have been more than enough for Thomas to believe that their report about the resurrection of Jesus was true.

But instead of chiding Thomas for wanting to see for himself, Jesus graciously gives Thomas the evidence he needs. While we are not afforded the same opportunity as Thomas in seeing Jesus' bodily resurrection, He still invites us to consider the overwhelming evidence that remains. We can look to Jesus' life and ministry for confirmation of our faith, as well as the faithful witness of the disciples, each of whose character is deserving of our trust. And when we do that, Jesus says, we can rest assured that "those who believe without seeing are blessed."

In what ways do you identify with Thomas when it comes to faith in Christ? Do you agree that "seeing is believing," or are you ready to trust that the resurrection of Jesus is true?

LIFE-CHANGING POWER OF THE GOSPEL

When I was struggling with my own doubts years ago, there was one thing I kept coming back to time and again, one thing that always seemed to strengthen my faith and reassure me that the things I believed in were true—and that was the changed lives of the disciples. There is no getting around the fact that Jesus' disciples were drastically changed following His resurrection. Prior to the resurrection, the biblical account of the disciples is far from flattering. On the night Jesus was betrayed and arrested, they abandoned their teacher in fear that a similar fate would fall upon them. In fact, we even see Peter, the bold leader of the pack so to speak, publicly deny any relationship with Jesus not once, not twice, but three times.

However, after Jesus appears to them we see a remarkable change as they finally realize exactly who He is. It is at this point that the disciples go from being timid, half-hearted followers to individuals willing to lay down their lives for the sake of sharing Christ's message with the world. In fact, history tells us that all of the disciples, with the exception of John who seemed to have died of natural causes, suffered a martyr's death. They were willing to undergo intense persecution to both themselves and their families—not to mention gruesome deaths—for their beliefs. It is hard to imagine that these individuals would persist through such horrific experiences for something they really didn't believe in, or for something that they thought even for a moment might be made up.

And while the changed lives of the disciples is always encouraging, the changed life of one of Christianity's greatest persecutors, the apostle Paul, is perhaps even more so. In Paul, we have the story of someone of who not only hated everything Christians believed and stood for, but actively hunted down and persecuted those who gave allegiance to Jesus. He would be thought of today as a religious radical given his zeal to persecute the church. However, such hatred would be radically transformed in Paul's life as he encountered the risen Christ on the road to Damascus.

From a worldly standard, Paul had everything going for him. He could boast of a long list of accolades and accomplishments that would cause most anyone to stop and take notice. Yet after meeting Jesus, Paul was fully convinced that all of these things were rubbish in comparison to knowing Christ (Phil. 3:8). His life was changed, and not just in the way that we think of Christians changing lifestyles today—changes in speech, changes in who we hang out with, changes in who we date, and so forth—but real change, as demonstrated through the sufferings he faced and persevered in. Paul was able to endure such things because he was fully convinced, beyond any doubt, that the gospel was indeed true.

It is for these reasons the changed lives of the disciples and the apostle Paul has always given me confidence during my own struggles with doubting. Perhaps their stories can be a source of confidence for you as well.

What was the point of Paul's boasting? How did it prove his love for Jesus?

Are they Hebrews? So am I. Are they Israelites? So am I. Are they the seed of Abraham? So am I. Are they servants of Christ? I'm talking like a madman—I'm a better one: with far more labors, many more imprisonments, far worse beatings, near death many times. Five times I received 39 lashes from Jews. Three times I was beaten with rods by the Romans. Once I was stoned by my enemies. Three times I was shipwrecked. I have spent a night and a day in the open sea. On frequent journeys, I faced dangers from rivers, dangers from robbers, dangers from my own people, dangers from the Gentiles, dangers in the city, dangers in the open country, dangers on the sea, and dangers among false brothers; labor and hardship, many sleepless nights, hunger and thirst, often without food, cold, and lacking clothing. Not to mention other things, there is the daily pressure on me: my care for all the churches.
—2 Cor. 11:22-28

FAITH AND THE SEARCH FOR CERTAINTY

Therefore, brothers, since we have boldness to enter the sanctuary through the blood of Jesus, by a new and living way He has opened for us through the curtain (that is, His flesh), and since we have a great high priest over the house of God, let us draw near with a true heart in full assurance of faith, our hearts sprinkled clean from an evil conscience and our bodies washed in pure water.

—Heb. 10:19-22

As a kid I remember wondering if everything I believed to be true—my day-to-day experiences, my family and friends, school, tests—were all just a part of an elaborate dream. I wondered, *What if I'm in a deep sleep and my entire life is one long movie being generated by my subconscious. What if everything I believe to be true about my life is, in fact, a make-believe story. Could I prove with absolute certainty that this scenario isn't really taking place?*

You may be thinking that sounds pretty far-fetched. But despite it's unlikelihood, most people enjoy imagining such unlikely scenarios. Movies like *Inception* and *The Matrix* series have made millions on the basic premise that the world as we know it may not actually be the real world but instead a constructed reality.

Of course, nobody loses sleep over it simply because there's no real reason to believe it could really happen. Even if we can't prove with certainty that life is not one long dream or isn't the product of being connected to a machine, we have no reason whatsoever to believe that such a strange scenario is true, yet many reasons that would lead us to conclude that life as we know it is, in fact, reality.

Faith is much the same way. As the author of Hebrews points out, we can have "full assurance" of faith in light of the fact that Jesus died on the cross for our sins and rose again to give us new life. It is a reason, among many others, we can point to as Christians that shows why it is more reasonable to believe than not to believe. This means that when it comes to dealing with personal doubts, it is important to remember that certainty isn't the end goal as Sean and I discussed in the interview, but rather full confidence and assurance that our faith has good reasons and evidences to sustain it. And when the evidence of Jesus' resurrection is considered, and the implications of what that fact means for us personally, then we can stand confidently knowing that our faith, indeed, is a reasonable faith, deserving of our trust and confidence.

How does it encourage you to know that you can approach Christ not only without guilt, but with full confidence that He will hear and respond to you?

SOMEONE WE CAN TRUST

Have you ever heard the story of Hiroo Onoda? Onoda was a Japanese imperial soldier who fought in WWII. He was trained as an intelligence officer and sent to the Philippine islands to thwart enemy invasion. In 1945 the United States and other allied forces landed on the island where Onoda and a few other soldiers were holding out. Under Onoda's orders, he and his soldiers retreated to the jungle that day for fear of being captured.

The most interesting thing about Onoda's story is the fact that he didn't come out of hiding for nearly 30 years. During that time, Onoda believed the war was still going on and that his original objective of fighting the enemy was still his mission. Even when allied forces dropped leaflets on the island explaining that the war had ended, Onoda and his fellow soldiers believed them to be propaganda, intended to draw them out for capture. Onoda needed something more to convince him that the war was indeed over. That would eventually come in the form of a visit from Onoda's original commanding officer, Major Yoshimi Taniguchi. In 1974, Yoshimi flew to the island and gave Onoda the official order that the war had ended and that he was to come out of hiding. And with that command from a trusted friend, Onoda relinquished his sword and firearm, and he finally surrendered.

I think about Onoda's story when I speak with someone who feels as if they are alone with their doubts and doesn't know who they can trust or turn to for help. Most of the time their feelings are a bit deceiving. After they begin talking, it turns out that there are people they can turn to, people they can trust with their personal struggles with doubting. It might be a parent, a youth pastor, or a trusted friend; the bottom line is, there is someone they can trust and someone who will listen.

Even though I encourage them to share and open up to someone in their life, my ultimate desire is to point them to Christ. You see, I'm fully convinced that when we get to know Jesus—when we encounter Him in the Gospels, when we read His words, when we consider the lives He changed—we can't help but trust in Him. Like Onoda trusting in a lifelong friend to convince him of the truth, we can look to Jesus and trust Him with our questions, knowing full well that not only is He deserving of our trust, but that He has all the answers we need.

Who is someone in your life you can turn to with your doubts? What steps will you take this week to begin a conversation about your faith and doubts with this person?

Simon Peter answered, "Lord, who will we go to? You have the words of eternal life."
—John 6:68

We have seen that having doubts and asking questions is a common experience for many people. Because we are finite beings with limited knowledge, we can expect doubts and questions to arise. Not only that, but having doubts and asking the tough questions isn't something we should feel shame over. As mentioned throughout the session, dealing with our doubts can cause us to not only grow and mature our faith, but can also equip us to be able to defend our faith to others.

AS YOU BEGIN TODAY'S STUDY, KEEP IN MIND THE FOLLOWING TAKEAWAYS FROM SESSION ONE:

» Many people struggle with doubts, and that is nothing to be ashamed over.

» Apologetics can help us address our doubts and provide the answers we and others need.

» Certainty is not required to know something is true—the goal is to have solid reasons and evidences that lead to a full assurance that our beliefs are true.

» The Christian faith isn't a blind faith, but rather one supported by good reasons and historical evidences.

Having dealt with the question of what we are to do with our doubts, we now turn to another big question: Does God really exist? The question of God's existence is at the foundation of all of other big questions, one that carries with it tremendous implications for how we think and live. If you've ever wondered whether there are good reasons to believe in God's existence, this session will help bring clarity to those lingering doubts you may be struggling with.

DOES GOD REALLY EXIST?

START

═══════════════════════»

┌─ SET THE SCENE ──────────────────────────────────

As you're scrolling through your social media news feed, you come across a
blog post written by a university professor that was shared by a friend of yours.
You click on the post and quickly notice that the main argument throughout
states that morality is relative—that there is no objective right or wrong—and
those that claim otherwise are trying to impose their morality on others. You
see that your friend has already left a comment in support of this position. How
do you respond?

WATCH

═══════════════════════»

FROM THE INTERVIEW

Cosmological Argument

   Step 1: Whatever begins to exist has a _____.

   Step 2: The _____ began to exist.

   Step 3: Therefore, the universe has a _____.

Moral Argument

   Step 1: If God does not _____, objective moral values and
      duties do not _____.

   Step 2: But _____ moral values and duties do exist.

   Step 3: Therefore, God _____.

Argument from Fine-Tuning

   Step 1: The fine-tuning of the universe is due to either physical

      _____, _____, or _____.

Step 2: It is not due to physical _____ or _____.

Step 3: Therefore, it is due to _____.

IN YOUR OWN WORDS

How would you explain the following arguments to someone?

Cosmological:

Moral:

Fine-tuning:

NOTES

In this section write down any additional thoughts, comments, or
questions related to the interview.

DISCUSS

How would you sum up the cosmological argument in your own words?

Why is it important to point out that creation isn't eternal but had a beginning?

If the world were just the product of natural forces, what implications would follow?

If the world were the product of a personal creator (which is what the evidence points us to), what implications would follow?

Summarize the moral argument in your own words.

Why is it difficult for the atheist to argue that morality is relative?

Imagine yourself back in time—all the way back to the year 1944. You are in Nazi Germany, and WWII is in full force. While most of the death around you is the direct result of national military forces warring with one another, you discover that another battle, one that is internal, is waging war for the soul of Germany itself— the Holocaust. You witness mass killings firsthand of those society has deemed inferior and biologically unfit to reproduce. You see the brutality displayed in these attempted exterminations by means of gunfire, poisonous gas, and massive oven chambers. And as you try to reason with the people of the day that such atrocities are absolutely wrong and should be stopped, those same people come back to you and say, "No, these acts aren't wrong because the culture deems them to be morally permissive."

In other words, if all of Germany thought what they were doing was acceptable, or even the rest of the world for that matter, would that have made it right? Explain.

What are some other moral issues that are not relative to time or culture?

1. racism

2. slavery

3. human rights

4.

5.

6.

Objective morals exist because an objective Moral Lawgiver exists—God. "I the LORD speak the truth; I declare what is right" (Isa. 45:19).

Read Romans 12:9.

> Love must be without hypocrisy. Detest evil; cling to what is good.

According to this passage, what does the Bible say with regard to the existence of objective good and evil? What should our response be?

FINE-TUNING ARGUMENTS

There are so many fine-tuning discoveries that have been made in recent years that it would be impossible to mention all of them here. Here are just two from the area of cosmology that completely do away with the notion that our universe is here by chance.

1. *Gravitational force constant* (large scale attractive force, holds people on planets and holds planets, stars, and galaxies together) If this is too weak, planets and stars cannot form; too strong, and stars burn up too quickly. As Dr. Craig mentions in the interview, if this were altered in less than 1 part in 10^{100}, life as we know it would not be possible.

2. *Cosmological constant* (which controls the expansion speed of the universe) This refers to the balance of the attractive force of gravity with a hypothesized repulsive force of space observable only at very large size scales. It must be very close to zero; that is, these two forces must be nearly perfectly balanced. To get the right balance, the cosmological constant must be fine-tuned to something like 1 part in 10^{120}. If it were just slightly more positive, the universe would fly apart; slightly negative, and the universe would collapse.

How big is a number like 1 in 10^{100}? Just in case you aren't aware, that is the number 10 with one hundred zeros following it. Mathematicians actually call this number googol.

So how long would it take for someone to count to one googol? Well, it would be impossible. Just to give you an idea on how big a number this is, think about this: Even if you were counting by two's, it would take you...

» 5 days, 18 hours, 53 minutes, 20 seconds non stop to count to one million.

» 15 years, 308 days, 6 hours, 53 minutes, 20 seconds non stop to count to one billion.

» $1.58 * 10^{92}$ years (or $1.58 * 10^{89}$ millennium) non-stop to count to one googol.

Like I said, you couldn't. In fact, the number googol is so high that there isn't even that many atoms in the entire universe!

I once heard a story from a philosopher asking us to imagine a conversation between two scientists following a successful space shuttle launch to the moon. "When the first moon rocket took off from Cape Canaveral, two scientists stood watching it, side by side. One was a believer, the other an unbeliever. The believer said, "Isn't it wonderful that our rocket is going to hit the moon by chance?" The unbeliever objected, "What do you mean, chance? We put millions of man hours of design into that rocket." "Oh," said the believer, "you don't think chance is a good explanation for the rocket? Then why do you think it's a good explanation for the universe? There's much more design in a universe than a rocket. We can design a rocket, but we couldn't design a whole universe. I wonder who can?"[1]

Why do you think it is difficult for some people to admit what seems obvious—that there is design all around us, and therefore there must be a Designer?

How might these arguments be helpful when conversing with those who are more scientific and/or philosophically minded?

What other arguments like these do you know of that could be used in talking with an unbeliever?

TRUE STORY

During graduate school I worked at a local YMCA. Many of my year-round co-workers were college students from nearby universities, and many more would join us during the summer months before heading back to school. Among these was a new guy, a sophomore student in college we will call Daniel, who was joining us for the summer break before returning to school.

My first day on the job with Daniel was entertaining to say the least. Daniel wasn't shy to express his beliefs, nor was he unwilling to defend them at all costs. The topic of that day: Is morality relative?

Daniel began discussing with other co-workers, who happened to be Christians, the issue of whether the moral beliefs we hold are objective (true regardless of whether anyone believes/practices them or not) or whether they were more aligned with individual preferences (along the lines of individual tastes, like cookies-and-cream versus mint chocolate chip). If they are objective, then everyone, no matter the time or culture in which they live, is obligated to follow them. If the latter, then people can just make their own decision or follow what culture deems appropriate when it comes to whether or not they will adhere to any particular moral belief system. Daniel was of the opinion that it was the latter.

When I arrived at work that day, other co-workers introduced me to Daniel and simply stated, "You guys need to talk." After hearing the context of the discussion, and after listening to what Daniel had to say, I asked Daniel if he could think of any time in history or culture in which it would be deemed appropriate to rape someone or torture children for fun if the cultural context allowed. He quickly, though hesitantly, responded by saying no. "Well, what about the holocaust?" I asked. It was the cultural belief of Nazi Germany that they were helping the evolutionary process along by exterminating millions of people they deemed to be inferior. "Was that morally permissible?" Again, Daniel responded by saying absolutely not.

I gave other examples that Daniel responded to with a resounding "no," making it clear that he didn't actually believe that all morality was relative. He intuitively knew, with the rest of us, that there are things that are objectively wrong, not dependent upon personal preference or culture. And once I was able to establish this fact, I was able to easily move into a discussion with Daniel as to where this objective morality is found—namely, in the character of God Himself, the Moral Lawgiver.

LOOK AND LISTEN

*The heavens declare the glory of God,
and the sky proclaims the work of His hands.
Day after day they pour out speech;
night after night they communicate knowledge.
There is no speech; there are no words;
their voice is not heard.
Their message has gone out to all the earth,
and their words to the ends of the world.
In the heavens He has pitched a tent for the sun.*
—Ps. 19:1-4

Having always lived near a big city, my view of the starry night sky has been limited due to all of the light coming from the streets and homes where I lived. Sure, I could occasionally sneak a peak at the grand light show in the sky, but my view of the stars and constellations was always dimmed on account of where I was. However, that all changed one summer when my wife and I visited Bryce Canyon National Park in Utah. Bryce Canyon, known for some of its incredible sand and clay structures, also happens to be one of the best places to stargaze in the United States. Because of its altitude and distance from any nearby light sources, people from all over bring their telescopes and binoculars for the chance to peer deep into the beauty that our solar system has to offer. It is a truly special place, and my experience of looking into the starry night sky there was nothing short of remarkable.

When I think back on those summer nights, camping under the stars at Bryce Canyon, the words of the psalmist come to mind. He talks about "the heavens" declaring the glory of God, meaning the stars, planets, and all that we see and are amazed at when we look up on a cloudless night. The heavenly wonders we've either seen with our own eyes or in pictures from the Hubble Telescope were created, according to the psalmist, to declare the glory of God. They "communicate knowledge" even though their communication is without words. It is the type of knowledge that comes by inference—similar to when you walk into your bedroom and notice that it has been picked up and everything is in its place, and you infer that someone else must have come in and cleaned it.

We draw inferences like this everyday. Some of them we get right, others we don't. The natural inference that comes to most people when taking in something as marvelous as the night sky is the conclusion that God created it. And not only is that the natural response, but it turns out that it is the best-supported one as well. After all, it is logically impossible for something to come into existence out of nothing. Physical things, like the universe, had a beginning at some point in the past. Not only that, but when we look to the created things, like the sky or places like the Grand Canyon, and listen to their inaudible speech like the psalmist did, we will see that the purpose for their existence is not merely to be admired by us, but to shine forth the glory of the One who created them.

What is the most impressive thing in nature you've seen? How do you respond when you see the amazing things God has created?

APART FROM GOD, THERE IS NO TRUTH

I have a friend who once visited Harvard University in order to be interviewed by their admissions department for entrance into the graduate program. While he was there the university arranged for him to be given a tour of the campus by a student who was currently enrolled at the time. At one point during the tour, my friend and his guide came across a place where the university's emblem was on display, which, if you have ever seen it, is a pretty simple logo with one Latin word front and center—veritas.

My friend, knowing a little Latin, asked the tour guide if she knew what that word meant. She admitted she did not, and so my friend went on to explain to her that it is the Latin word for "truth." Without much surprise, the young lady gave a polite "huh" and they resumed their tour.

I share this to remind ourselves of the importance of truth in this day and age. It wasn't too long ago that our culture, along with other cultures in the Western world, went through a period of believing that truth was relative—meaning truth was not something out there to be known and grasped, but was rather something that you made it to be for yourself. Because of the philosophical schools of thought at that time, people began to think of truth in a completely subjective sense, meaning something that is true for one person may not be true for another.

Now, this notion that all truth is relative has gone away for the most part, largely on account of the logical absurdity and impracticality of living out that belief. Think about it: If you say that truth is relative, then the claim that truth is relative must be relative as well; and if that is the case, why would I have any reason to believe you. Not only that, but try living out the belief that truth is relative. You can't. You make decisions every day based on what you believe to be true—you're careful around heights because you believe that the truth about gravity is real, or you're careful to avoid eating rat poison because you believe that the truth about it making you sick is real. So not only is the belief that truth is relative logically contradictory, but it is also unlivable.

Truth is important because without God, there would be no objective grounds for truth. Truth exists because God exists. And while there may remain pockets of people in our culture today who try to deny the existence of truth, they do so despite all of the evidence pointing us to the belief that truth is real. Like Pilate, they wonder what truth is, even when the face of Truth is right in front of them.

> Do most people today live as though truth is a matter of opinion or as though it's absolute? Why is it important to know that Jesus is truth and speaks truth? How does this affect your trust in Him?

"You are a king then?" Pilate asked.

"You say that I'm a king," Jesus replied. "I was born for this, and I have come into the world for this: to testify to the truth. Everyone who is of the truth listens to My voice."

"What is truth?" said Pilate.

After he had said this, he went out to the Jews again and told them, "I find no grounds for charging Him. You have a custom that I release one prisoner to you at the Passover. So, do you want me to release to you the King of the Jews?"
—**John 18:37-39**

APART FROM GOD, THERE IS NO JUSTICE

Here is My Servant whom I have chosen, My beloved in whom My soul delights; I will put My Spirit on Him, and He will proclaim justice to the nations.
—Matt. 12:18

Recently the entertainment industry has found a great deal of success in developing programs around the notion of injustices within America's criminal justice system. Programs like NPR's "Serial" and Netflix's "Making a Murderer" have attracted millions of viewers by posing one simple question: Have the people prosecuted in these cases been unjustly convicted of their crimes?

The question, though simple, is something just about everyone finds fascinating given that we all have an innate sense of what justice is and should look like, as well as a moral distaste when we witness injustice. When we turn on the nightly news or check social media, we are bombarded with stories of how people have treated—or rather mistreated—others. We see stories of mass destruction and bombings from terrorists, stories of genocide or even gendercide taking place in other parts of the world. And while certainly being hurt by these things and feeling empathy for the people involved, we also feel just as strongly that justice should be served and that such terrible injustices should be stopped.

As Christians, we know that with the fall in Genesis 3, our world became broken because of sin. And because of this brokenness, we see too often that justice does not always prevail. The culprit is not caught or the act goes unpunished. It would seem as though sometimes there are no consequences for wicked actions and that it doesn't matter whether one chooses good or evil.

If God did not exist, then ultimate justice would not exist either, and our world would be a very sad place indeed. Thankfully, God's existence gives us the assurance that our lives do have a purpose and that our actions do matter. We desire that justice be administered because we serve a God who always does what is good and right. Even when we witness unjust acts taking place, as Christians we can be encouraged to live justly, resting in the truth that one day God will set all things right.

Have you ever been angry over an injustice? Why should some things that are taking place in our world make us angry? Why should believers be involved in fighting injustice? What should our motivation be?

APART FROM GOD, THERE IS NO GOODNESS

A few years ago my wife and I visited the Holocaust Museum in Washington D.C. If you've ever been then you're familiar with the intense imagery that surrounds you as you tour the museum. I'll never forget the piles of shoes, clothes, and other personal items, each representing a unique life that was brutally punished and eventually killed. The pictures and stories of those in concentration camps can be quite overwhelming as you begin to grasp the intense evil of the holocaust.

Even though it is a sobering museum to walk through, it is helpful in that it allows you to travel back to the time of Nazi Germany. Think about it: The year is 1941 and you are living in one of the worst concentration camps during that time—Auschwitz. All around you is the smell, sight, and fear of death. There you are in the heart of the holocaust where the presence of evil is so overwhelming you are stricken with terror. During that time you witness the murder of over one million people, many of them friends and family, killed because they were hated for their race, religious beliefs, or even for their physical appearance.

There are many emotions that arise when you walk through a museum like this one. Hurt, anger, disgust, and sadness, for sure, but also the belief that such acts were undoubtedly morally wrong. Despite some people who may seem to have no moral compass and don't believe in the existence of good and evil, nearly all of us would say with absolute assurance that such acts were evil and wrong.

This is important because apart from God, the concept and reality of goodness would not exist. In other words, apart from having a moral lawgiver whose character is completely good, we would be unable to say with any authority that such acts are either good or bad, right or wrong. All morality would be relative—good for some, perhaps bad for others. We would be unable to say that acts of terrorism are wrong, or that torturing infants for fun an act of evil. Of course, the very thought of horrific things like that not being declared evil and wrong is unsettling to us, and rightly so. Why? Because objective goodness does exist because God does exist. And though evil may prevail for a time, as Christians we take refuge in Jesus, who promises that one day He will wipe away every tear, making all wrongs right as He makes all things new again (Revelation 21:4).

Does someone's choice not to acknowledge God's goodness make it any less true? Why or why not? In what ways has God proven His goodness to you personally?

Again, I observed all the acts of oppression being done under the sun. Look at the tears of those who are oppressed; they have no one to comfort them. Power is with those who oppress them; they have no one to comfort them. So I admired the dead, who have already died, more than the living, who are still alive. But better than either of them is the one who has not yet existed, who has not seen the evil activity that is done under the sun.
—Eccl. 4:1-3

APART FROM GOD, LIFE HAS NO MEANING

I increased my achieve-ments. I built houses and planted vineyards for myself. I made gardens and parks for myself and planted every kind of fruit tree in them. I constructed reservoirs of water for myself from which to irrigate a grove of flourishing trees. I acquired male and female servants and had slaves who were born in my house. I also owned many herds of cattle and flocks, more than all who were before me in Jerusalem. I also amassed silver and gold for myself, and the treasure of kings and provinces. I gathered male and female singers for myself, and many concubines, the delights of men. So I became great and surpassed all who were before me in Jerusalem; my wisdom also remained with me. All that my eyes desired, I did not deny them. I did not refuse myself any pleasure, for I took pleasure in all my struggles. This was my reward for all my struggles. When I considered all that I had accomplished and what I had labored to achieve, I found everything to be futile and a pursuit of the wind. There was nothing to be gained under the sun.

—Eccl. 2:4-11

Have you ever asked the question, "Does life have meaning?" Have you ever wondered whether there is purpose to your existence? The question about the meaning of life is nothing new, of course. Individuals have been asking the same question for centuries.

To begin answering this question, however, one needs to first settle the question concerning God's existence. Why? Because the question about whether life has meaning is directly tied to whether God exists. This idea was illustrated somewhat recently by the late atheist Christopher Hitchens, who was once asked in a debate, "If God does not exist, what then is the purpose and meaning to life?" In typical glib and sarcastic humor, Hitchens replied, "Well, I can only answer for myself. Whatever cheers me up. I suppose mainly gloating over the misfortunes of other people." He then went on to list other things, such as irony and sex, before saying that everyone is making a "clear run to the grave."[2]

Why would Hitchens respond this way? Is this the standard answer of the self-professing atheist? It would seem that an answer along these lines would certainly follow from the atheistic worldview. This is because, as Hitchens well knew, if God does not exist then the objective grounds for ultimate meaning and purpose do not exist either.

By acknowledging God's existence one also acknowledges the existence of meaning and purpose within the universe. True meaning can only come from a personal Creator who has endowed creation with meaning and significance. As the philosopher Tom Morris has said, "We can create islands of meaning in this sea of existence we've been given, but it is beyond the power of any of us to endow with meaning the entirety of life itself or the entirety of any of our own lives."[3]

There are vast implications to the worldviews around us. Only by affirming God can one coherently support the notion that life is endowed with meaning and purpose. It is only in a being like God, as Tom Morris puts it, "a creator of all who could eventually, in the words of the New Testament, 'work all things together for good'—only this sort of being could guarantee a completeness and permanency of meaning for human lives."[4]

In your opinion, what gives life real meaning? How do the things you find meaning in influence your belief in God?

WHAT ABOUT BEAUTY?

This question may sound a little strange to you, but have you ever been moved by something beautiful? Have you ever been in awe while standing on the edge of the Grand Canyon, or overwhelmed looking up at the Milky Way on a dark and cloudless night? Have you ever watched a newborn baby, amazed at the beauty of life? Or have you ever been fascinated seeing a favorite animal for the first time in person? Whatever the situation, it is probably safe to assume to that you have been moved by something beautiful.

C. S. Lewis used to talk and write about how humans long to experience beauty to some degree or another. In fact, according to him, it is as if we were made to experience it. But the longing and search for beauty, according to Lewis, is actually a search for the source of that beauty. For Lewis, the source of the beauty is never completely contained within the objects or moments that we find beautiful—it only comes through them as the cable in your own home comes through the television set. He says, "The books or the music in which we thought the beauty was located will betray us if we trust to them; it was not in them, it only came through them, and what came through them was longing. These things—the beauty, the memory of our own past—are good images of what we really desire; but if they are mistaken for the thing itself they turn into dumb idols, breaking the hearts of their worshipers. For they are not the thing itself; they are only the scent of a flower we have not found, the echo of a tune we have not heard, news from a country we have never yet visited."[5]

This longing for beauty, significance, and meaning that seems to be present within each of us only makes sense if God exists. If God doesn't exist, then these things are nothing but illusions caused by chemical reactions taking place within the brain. But since we have overwhelming support to believe that God does exist, then we can also believe that these things—these moments of being moved by beauty—are actually designed by Him to draw our attention beyond the earthly object to the source of where that beauty lies, which is in Him. As the early church father St. Augustine once said, "You [God] have made us for you, and our heart is restless until it finds its rest in you."[6] All beauty and longing and meaning point our attention upward to Him, the very object of our heart's desires.

> When have you found yourself pausing to reflect on the beauty of creation? Have you taken time to see His work as a testimony of His existence?

He has made everything appropriate in its time. He has also put eternity in their hearts, but man cannot discover the work God has done from beginning to end.
—Eccl. 3:11

Splendor and majesty are before Him; strength and beauty are in His sanctuary.
—Ps. 96:6

We have looked at three distinct, yet powerful arguments for why belief in God's existence is both reasonable and supported by the best evidences that we have. The Cosmological, Moral, and Fine-Tuning Arguments all demonstrate that what we know about the universe and ourselves points to the existence of a Creator who is distinct from His creation. These arguments not only serve to strengthen our own faith and overcome the doubts we may have, but they are effective tools in defending the faith to others by appealing to sources of authority that they likely will accept (sources like philosophy, science, and moral intuition).

AS YOU BEGIN TODAY'S STUDY, KEEP IN MIND THE FOLLOWING TAKEAWAYS FROM SESSION TWO:

» The Cosmological argument demonstrates the universe isn't eternal but was brought into being.

» The Moral argument demonstrates that the existence of objective morality points to an objective Moral Lawgiver.

» The Fine-tuning argument demonstrates that an intelligent mind brought the universe into being, having designed it with the specific intention of making it a habitable place for life to exist.

Of course, there are dozens of other reasons and evidences we could point to in order to support our belief in God's existence (some of which are mentioned in the devotions for that session). However, it is clear that belief in God's existence is a well-supported belief to hold, making it more reasonable to believe than not to believe. Having tackled this, we now turn to the topic of science and whether or not science is at odds with our Christian faith.

IS THERE CONFLICT BETWEEN FAITH AND SCIENCE?

START

»

SET THE SCENE

You're working on a group project for science class on the origin of the universe. One of the group members, a classmate you don't know very well, makes the off-hand comment that Christians are ignorant for believing in God when it is obvious that natural causes are sufficient enough to account for the existence of the universe as we know it. How do you respond?

WATCH

»

FROM THE INTERVIEW

Interaction between Christianity and science has not been a _____.

Science has discovered that the universe is _____, delicately balanced so that life could appear.

Information always comes from an _____ _____.

It takes an _____ _____ to explain irreducible complexity.

Science itself provides overwhelming _____ for belief in God.

IN YOUR OWN WORDS

Explain how the Christian worldview provided the very foundation for science to be practiced.

Summarize the concept of irreducible complexity and why it is important.

How would you explain to someone that science is supportive of Christianity?

NOTES

In this section write down any additional thoughts, comments, or questions related to the interview.

DISCUSS

What comes to mind when you think about the relationship between science and religion?

How does your perception of this relationship match up to the way this discussion is often presented in culture?

Have you ever felt like you had to choose between science or your faith? If so, why?

What stood out to you the most during the video interview for this session? Explain.

In looking at the history of science, why is it important to note that the Christian worldview paved the way for the scientific enterprise?

DESIGN IS ALL AROUND US

How is design seen in other fields of investigation?

SETI:

Detectives:

Archaeologists:

Insurance companies:

Cryptologists:

Discoveries from cosmology to biology reveal not only our universe, but how humans are so intricately designed that to believe it all happened by chance would require one to have way more faith than that of a Christian. Consider a few fine-tuning conditions relating to just our planet.

1. If the earth were merely 1 percent closer to the sun, the oceans would vaporize, preventing the existence of life.

2. If our planet were just 2 percent farther from the sun, the oceans would freeze.

3. We must have a large moon with right planetary rotation (which stabilizes a planet's tilt and contributes to tides). In the case of Earth, the gravitational pull of its moon stabilizes the angle of its axis at a nearly constant 23.5 degrees. This ensures relatively temperate seasonal changes and the only climate in the solar system mild enough to sustain complex living organisms.

For the experts who are studying in these fields and following the evidence where it leads, what should they conclude about these findings?

Years ago there was a talk show host who would conduct interviews on the street, asking random people very basic questions. It was fun to laugh when people didn't know the answers, or when they would make up an answer that was incredibly ridiculous. On one episode, the host asked participants how Mt. Rushmore was formed (you know, the mountain that has the faces of four of our most popular presidents carved on the side). One participant responded with "erosion." Caught off-guard, the talk show host clarified, "Okay, you're telling me that the faces of four famous presidents were carved into the side of a mountain by the natural forces of wind and rain?" And with that, the interviewee responded with a resounding, "Yes!"

WHAT ABOUT EVOLUTION?

When it comes to evolution, here are some pointers to help you navigate the landscape. People naturally assume that the term "evolution" can only have one meaning, but that's far from true. Evolution can be broken down the following ways:

1. *Evolution:* This can broadly refer to merely change over time or any sequence of events in nature.

2. *Microevolution:* This refers to minor changes and variations within a species, such as the different finch beaks discovered on the Galapagos islands.

3. *Macroevolution:* Large-scale changes resulting in a new and distinct species.

   a. *natural selection*: the blind, undirected, and purposeless process that is believed to be sufficient in accounting for the origin and diversity of life

   b. *common descent*: the belief that all organisms have descended from a single common ancestor

   c. *random mutation*: the mechanism used by natural selection in determining which mutations and/or variations would give an advantage to a species, as well as which ones will not

 IS THERE CONFLICT BETWEEN FAITH AND SCIENCE?   **39**

Why is it important to define what we mean by "evolution" in an apologetic conversation?

What scientific evidence is there to support the idea of microevoution? macroevolution?

Macroevolution is driven more by worldview than by science and scientific discoveries. If someone with an atheistic worldview already accepts the belief that God doesn't exist, then he or she will assume that nature is self-sufficient in accounting for life as we know it. They will look at the evidence and try to interpret it to fit their preconceived beliefs about God. Thus, their conclusions are driven more from their theological beliefs than their scientific ones.

Science is not an enemy—it never has been nor is it today. Even atheist Stephen Jay Gould, widely regarded as America's greatest evolutionary biologist, was adamant that his own skepticism could not be derived from the sciences. He says:

> "To say it for all my colleagues and for the umpteenth million time... science simply cannot (by its legitimate methods) adjudicate the issue of God's possible superintendence of nature. We neither affirm nor deny it; we simply can't comment on it as scientists."[1]

WHERE DOES JESUS FIT IN?

For hundreds of years, philosophers have wondered how everything holds together. What is at the essence of things? What is it that unites all things together? Speaking to philosophers at the Areopagus, the apostle Paul answered this question when he said:

> "Therefore, what you worship in ignorance, this I proclaim to you. The God who made the world and everything in it—He is Lord of heaven and earth and does not live in shrines made by hands. Neither is He served by human hands, as though He needed anything, since He Himself gives everyone life and breath and all things. From one man He has made every nationality to live over the whole earth and has determined their appointed times and the boundaries of where they live. He did this so they might seek God, and perhaps they might reach out and find Him, though He is not far from each one of us. For in Him we live and move and exist." —Acts 17:23-28

"In Him we live and move and exist." The answer to the age-old question of what unites all things and holds all things together, according to Paul, is Christ. All things were created through Him and for Him. We can investigate things like atoms and quarks, but in the end none of these things will make sense apart from the Creator.

TRUE STORY

Not too long ago I was speaking at a winter retreat for a high school student ministry. During the second day of the retreat, the youth pastor invited me to an informal "Question and Answer" time with the students. Having really enjoyed doing these in the past with other youth groups, I enthusiastically agreed to participate.

When the session started, the youth pastor opened the floor to anyone who had questions. As soon as the invitation was extended, hands went up all over the room. The first student who was called on asked a series of question having to do with science and faith, such as: "Does science contradict faith?" "What about evolution is true?" "What about the Big Bang?"

I was grateful for the student's questions and answered them one by one. Of course, this was certainly not the only time I have had the opportunity to discuss the relationship between science and faith. These opportunities come up frequently. However, I share this example with you simply to show how students today, your own peers, are wrestling with this very topic. They have questions, and to be quite honest, many of them feel as if they don't have anyone to turn to for answers.

What an encouragement it is to know that you can be the very help that many of your friends need when it comes to answering these types of questions. You can shed light on the history of science and Christianity, talk about the various and often misunderstood ways that evolution is talked about, or share with them the cutting-edge discoveries that point to an intelligent design within creation. And when the answers go beyond your own understanding, you can not only point them in the direction of helpful books and talks by some of the experts, but you can also come alongside of them in the attempt to find the answers together.

WHAT IS SCIENCE?

Now the earth was formless and empty, darkness covered the surface of the watery depths, and the Spirit of God was hovering over the surface of the waters.

—Gen. 1:2

After having completed an M.A. in philosophy of science, I can tell you firsthand that the history of science is much more complex than what most people think. For starters, science is one of those things that is nearly impossible to define. There are some standard entry-level textbooks that try to define science in accordance with the scientific method of investigating the natural world using skills like observation and experimentation. While it is helpful to turn to the standard method used among scientists; unfortunately, this doesn't help much given that not all of the sciences use the same methods. Cosmologists, astronomers, geologists, biologists, microbiologists, chemists, biochemists, and physicists explore different parts of creation using different methods. This is because the nature of what is being studied will always determine the way it is studied.

Perhaps most remarkable when it comes to the history of science is the fact that modern-day science (the approach to science that came out of Renaissance Europe) was born out of the Christian worldview. The Christian worldview provided the framework for science to operate, which is why the majority of the early great scientists were believers. They believed not only that the Creator of the universe was orderly and rational, but that His creation displayed those same characteristics as well, making science possible. If things were not orderly, then there would be no regularity within nature, and if no regularity, then no science. Not only that, but these early Christian scientists, as well as scientists today, were in awe of the fact that the human mind was capable of discerning this ordering. Theoretical physicist John Polkinghorne has said: "We are so familiar with the fact that we can understand the world that most of the time we take it for granted. It is what makes science possible. Yet it could have been otherwise. The universe might have been a disorderly chaos rather than an orderly cosmos. Or it might have had a rationality which was inaccessible to us... There is a congruence between our minds and the universe, between the rationality experienced within and the rationality observed without."[2]

Like Polkinghorne said, we do take this simple fact for granted. But when you do think about it, things could be really different. No only that, but given certain worldviews one would expect things to be quite different. It is as if God designed us with this very capacity to see the mathematical precision and elegance of the universe He has designed. All of this would suggest that looking into nature and investigating the world God has designed is not only natural to the way God designed us, but also healthy in that it points us beyond the beauty of His creation to the greater beauty of the Creator Himself.

Why is it important to understand that everything started with God?

WHAT DO THE FACTS TELL US?

There is one important thing you should always remember when it comes to evaluating a scientific claim: facts do not interpret themselves. I know, that may sound weird and insignificant, but it is a hugely important notion.

Think of it this way: The things we observe within nature, the things we see and feel and examine under microscopes, are the things we call the facts. Imagine a crime scene investigator arriving at the scene of a homicide. He might look at the condition of the house the victim is in (Is it trashed with signs of forced entry or does it look like nothing has been touched?), the condition and position of the body (Was there a struggle?), where the murder weapon might be, and if there are any clues as to who else was in the home (fingerprints, DNA, etc.). All of the things he looks at are the "facts," the information he has to work with. But if you think about it, the facts are not self-interpreting. It takes a mind to piece together the facts and draw proper inferences, such as the possibility that the victim knew his attacker because there are no signs of forced entry and no signs of a struggle.

This is what we mean when we say that facts are not self-interpreting. In order to make sense, they require an intelligent mind, and that mind may or may not arrive at the right conclusions. We don't always reason correctly or draw all the right inferences is because we bring with us our own set of assumptions or presuppositions when looking at the evidence. Think about it: Has there ever been a time when you read into someone's behavior and actions, maybe someone at church or school that you really liked, and imagined the reason for those actions must be because they feel the same way? You wanted to believe they felt the same way, and because of that you looked at the facts and interpreted his or her actions through that lens. However, it is all too often the case that feelings get hurt in these situations because one person "read into" the facts things that weren't really there.

The same is true when it comes to science. Not only do the facts not interpret themselves, but as observers we have to be careful not to bring the wrong presuppositions to the scientific process. For instance, if we were to begin our understanding of science with the presupposition that God didn't exist, and that everything within nature can be explained by other natural processes (by the way, this is called "methodological naturalism" and many scientists use it all the time), then from the very outset we have made it impossible for some potential explanations to even be considered. If we have the presupposition that only mindless matter exists, then we are forced to exclude from the start any notion of God or His intervention within human history. But this, of course, isn't science. This is an atheistic worldview trying to use science for its own advantage. Instead, science follows the evidence where the evidence leads, whether pointing to the natural, or perhaps even the supernatural.

Why do you believe God does or doesn't exist? Is your belief based on your own research or wrapped up in what others have told you?

For I passed on to you as most important what I also received:

that Christ died for our sins according to the Scriptures,

that He was buried,

that He was raised on the third day according to the Scriptures,

and that He appeared to Cephas,

then to the Twelve.

Then He appeared to over 500 brothers at one time;

most of them are still alive, but some have fallen asleep.

Then He appeared to James,

then to all the apostles.

Last of all, as to one abnormally born,

He also appeared to me.
—1 Cor. 15:3-8

A FINE-TUNED UNIVERSE

*For it was You who
created my inward parts;*

*You knit me together in
my mother's womb.*

*I will praise You because
I have been remarkably
and wonderfully made.*

*Your works are wonderful,
and I know this very well.*

—Ps. 139:13-14

The Christian worldview clearly states that we are here—that our universe is here—by the purposeful intention and design of our Creator. Not by chance or necessity, but by design. But how does that notion settle with science? Does science support that belief, or does it call it into question?

You heard in the video that scientists have made a number of discoveries over the years that fall under the category of what they often call "fine-tuning." In essence, fine-tuning states that scientific discoveries from cosmology to biology all reveal not only our universe, but how we ourselves are so intricately designed that to believe it all happened by chance would require way more faith than even that of a Christian.

To apply this notion of chance to just one of the fine-tuning examples cosmologists have discovered, consider this example by astrophysicist Hugh Ross. In talking about the ratio between the electromagnetic force-constant to the gravitational force-constant and their need to be delicately balanced, an increase by only 1 part in 10^{40} would mean only small stars can exist, and a decrease by the same amount would mean there would only be large stars—important because you must have both large and smalls stars in the universe. Ross helps us conceive of the possibility of this happening by chance by telling us to imagine covering America with coins in a column reaching to the moon (236,000 miles away), then doing the same for a billion other continents of the same size. Paint one coin red and put it somewhere in one of the billion piles. Then blindfold a friend and ask her to pick out the red coin. The odds are about 1 in 10^{40} that she will.[3]

Now, that is truly an astronomical number. If you began writing out the zeros of this number now and didn't stop for the rest of your natural life, you still wouldn't come close to finishing. That's how big a number it is! And this is just one example of the universe's fine-tuning that scientists have discovered, all of which point us to the inevitable conclusion that we are not here by chance, but by design.

In what ways does knowing that you were intentionally and uniquely created by God impact your worldview?

DEFINING EVOLUTION

Whether in high school science or on a BBC nature documentary, the theory of evolution is the standard scientific view for how life began. In fact, it's so embedded within the larger scientific community that it is often taken for granted—people assume it's true and that there's no reason to question it. Of course, those who do question it or offer alternative explanations are deemed religious fanatics in disguise and traitors to their scientific practice. The community might expect such criticism from those with little to no science background, labeling them ignorant and religiously blinded. However, it stings a little more when they see their prestigious peers, many of whom are leaders in their field, question the validity of evolutionary theory and its role in the diversity of life.

When it comes the topic of evolution, it's important to define terms. People naturally assume that the term "evolution" can only have one meaning and that everyone is using it in that sense. But this is far from true. (Refer back to the Discuss section for a full list of definitions.)

When it comes to understanding and/or critiquing an argument for evolution, it's important to know which aspect of evolution is being discussed. The standard examples in support of evolution in high school textbooks fall under the first category of microevolution. Whether it be the finches' beaks or the peppered moth, these examples show how small, minuscule changes can take place in order to help organisms adapt. However, this aspect of evolution isn't the one Christian scientists are concerned about. It is easy to believe, given our own knowledge about God and the world He created, that there is built-in variation and adaption for organisms. However, in no way does it follow that since small changes are possible within a species that large-scale ones must be as well. It is in this area of macroevolution that evolution is highly contested in the scientific community. Why? Because large-scale macroevolutionary change necessary to assemble new organs or body plans requires, according to many biologists, the creation of entirely new genetic information—information which much be present from the beginning.

> What difference does it make in how you approach life if you know you were created by God?

In the beginning was the Word,

and the Word was with God,

and the Word was God.

He was with God in the beginning.

All things were created through Him,

and apart from Him not one thing was created

that has been created.

—John 1:1-3

All things were created through Him, and apart from Him not one thing was created that has been created.

—John 1:3

WHAT DID DARWIN SAY?

During my graduate studies I was required to read Charles Darwin's *The Origin of Species*, in which he argues the existence of natural selection and common descent as the explanation for the diversity of life. In other words, there's no need for God since nature can evolve on its own.

One of the statements Darwin made is quite eye-opening. He said, "If it could be demonstrated that any complex organ existed, which could not possibly have been formed by numerous, successive, slight modifications, my theory would absolutely break down."[4] He believed that natural selection causes the slight changes and modifications that, over an extended time, give rise to new species. He added that if there are complex organs that could not have gradually evolved by means of natural selection, then his theory would be discredited. The year was 1859.

Fast-forward to today with advanced microscopes, knowledge of everything about the cell, and the volumes of information encoded into just one strand of DNA. As science continues to progress, many scientists have abandoned Darwin's theory of natural selection on the basis of his own test that there are obvious organs that demonstrate what is called "irreducible complexity." Irreducible complexity basically states that organs do exist that could not have evolved over a long period of time given that all of their parts would have to have been in place, in the right order, from the very beginning. There are many examples of irreducible complexity, one being the bacterial flagellum found within a human cell. The flagellum is a remarkable organ comprised of over 40 distinct parts, and it looks and operates like an on-board motor engine. It is, in the words of many microbiologists, a micro-machine whose sophistication is unlike anything the best engineers in the world could produce. The 40 parts to make this engine operate must not only be present, but assembled in the right order. If just one part is missing, the flagellum won't work, or if all the parts are there but not arranged properly, then once again it would be inoperable.

Why did Darwin believe that something like the flagellum would be enough to undermine his entire theory? Because natural selection works by a long and gradual process, conferring advantages to a species by selecting which features and changes it needs in order to survive. When it comes to the flagellum, however, natural selection would be unable to account for its existence since all parts must be present and in order from the beginning—in other words, it is irreducibly complex. Natural selection couldn't have collected the parts and stored them for later use given that natural selection, according to evolutionary theorists, discards things that do not confer an advantage to the species.

There are many scientific examples of irreducible complexity that make belief in natural selection problematic, the information contained in DNA being one. While the conversation between scientists continues to take place in this area, however, you can be equipped to follow along as science continues to reveal design within our biological world.

In what ways does the complexity of things like bacterial flagellum point to God as our Creator?

WHEN SCIENCE AND
WORLDVIEWS COLLIDE

Have you ever heard about the eugenics movement that took place in the early to mid 20th century? While America was rightly condemning the horrific nature of the holocaust taking place in Nazi Germany, it faced its own ethical decisions that would bring embarrassment to its history books.

In short, the eugenics movement was a way to carry out the social implications of a Darwinian worldview—the belief that evolutionary processes, by means of natural selection, would lead to a stronger human race. It was embraced by scientists, social thinkers, and physicians, and it eventually led to state policies and procedures that carried implications for millions of Americans. Those applying for marriage had to be examined by a physician to determine physical and mental health. Children received eugenic testing to determine aptitude, eventually directing the course of their education and/or trade. And tens of thousands would receive forced sterilizations as the result of being deemed hereditarily unfit.

In short, the practice of eugenics was an attempt by some to control human breeding. And while most European and American scientists considered eugenics "scientific," it fell out of favor soon after it became well-known what the Nazi's were doing with eugenic practices. Of course, this was only well after more than 60,000 people who were considered "defectives" in America received forced sterilization, people who would not be characterized as such by today's modern standards of mental health.

It was not a shining moment for American history by any means. But was science to blame? Was scientific progress the enemy here? Science wasn't the enemy, but just simply the tool people used to justify their actions. Science is a neutral endeavor, used by both moral and immoral people. And while it has often been used for the good of humanity—as seen in medications and surgical procedures—it has also been used by some to commit some of the worst atrocities known in human history.

> What is the ultimate danger in living according to anything other than a biblical worldview?

There is a way that seems right to a man, but its end is the way to death.
—Prov. 14:12

We have seen that when it comes to the issue of science and faith, there are many people today who propose that science and faith are at war with each other. However, we've also seen that there is a rich and fruitful history with Christianity and science, the former actually serving as the very intellectual foundation for the latter. And while the two are often very separate things, when they do overlap we discover that science is overwhelmingly supportive of the Christian worldview, having made discoveries and insights that point to an intelligent Designer of creation.

AS YOU BEGIN TODAY'S STUDY, KEEP IN MIND THE FOLLOWING TAKEAWAYS FROM SESSION THREE:

» Science and faith are allies, not enemies.

» Scientific discoveries in recent decades support the belief in God's existence.

» Those who try to use science to argue against God are actually imposing their atheistic beliefs into their practice of science.

» Signs of intelligent design are all around us, from the discoveries in cosmology to those in biology.

Having settled the question of whether science is in conflict with faith, we now turn our attention to another big question: What about other world religions?

WHAT ABOUT OTHER WORLD RELIGIONS?

START

»

SET THE SCENE

You and a friend are sitting at your house watching a late-night talk show. On this particular evening, one of the guest appearances happens to be a well-known politician who is running for re-election. The host begins to ask the guest about some of the different views and policies he holds, and one of the issues that comes up is religion. The politician responds by saying, "I'm more of a pluralist when it comes to religious belief, meaning I think all religions are pretty much the same when you think about it. Consider this analogy to explain what I mean: Imagine seeing an elephant and six blind men. The first blind man walks up to the elephant and grabs the tusk and says, "It is a spear!" The second feels the trunk and concludes, "It is a snake!" The third hugs the leg and says, "It is a tree!" The one touching the tail claims, "It is a rope!" Another feeling the ear states, "It is a fan!" And finally, the last blind man feels the elephant's side and concludes, "It is a wall!"

The politician goes on to express that religious beliefs can be viewed in much the same way. Each blind man, representing a different religion, only grasps a small bit of the big picture—of ultimate reality. They have a handle on it somewhat, and they do the best they can to describe it, but in the end, they are essentially talking about the same thing.

After hearing that, your friend turns to you and says, "That makes sense!" How do you respond?

WATCH

»

FROM THE INTERVIEW

The problem being solved in Christianity is the _____ that separates human beings from God.

Salvation as a free gift from God is one of the _____ features of Christianity.

Christianity isn't just a _____ among all of the world religions. It's a unique _____ of the world.

Christianity is _____.

The _____ of Jesus is one of the best-attested facts of the ancient world.

IN YOUR OWN WORDS

How would you explain to someone that not all religions are the same?

What are some ways Christianity is unique among the world religions?

How would you explain to someone the uniqueness of Jesus compared to other religious leaders?

NOTES

In this section write down any additional thoughts, comments, or questions related to the interview.

DISCUSS

═══════════════════════════════⟫

What did you find interesting about the video interview?

What other religious beliefs have you been exposed to?

How have you thought about other religions in the past?

What do you think is the typical cultural attitude toward other world religions, especially as it is reflected in movies, music, and other art forms?

What does the existence of world religions tell us about ourselves?

THE UNIQUENESS OF JESUS

Jesus is often seen as a universal religious figure, meaning that numerous religions try to adopt Jesus and make Him one of their own. For instance, some Hindus think that Jesus might very well be an avatar of Vishnu, that is, a reincarnation of that particular Hindu deity. In fact, Gandhi, one of Hindu's most well-known teachers, believed that Jesus was one of the greatest religious teachers of all time.

In Islam, Jesus is said to not only be a prophet like Muhammad, but also that He was born of a virgin, was a legitimate miracle worker, and that He will stand with Allah at the scales of justice at the end of time. In other words, he is a very prominent figure even among Muslims.

However, even though many religions appreciate Jesus and His teachings, it is clear that all of these religions fail to acknowledge the truth of who Jesus claimed to be—God in flesh. They appreciate Jesus' teachings on love and grace, but they completely ignore the rest of Scripture that talks about Jesus' identity as the incarnate Son of God who came to save and rescue us when we were completely unable to rescue ourselves. Yes, Jesus is loving, and He talked a great deal about what it means to love God and one's neighbor. But Jesus is also the One who will one day judge humanity and make all things right again.

What are some other religions that fail to acknowledge the truth of Jesus' person and work?

How does the resurrection demonstrate Jesus' uniqueness among the leaders of other religions?

WORKS VERSUS GRACE

Read Proverbs 4:23 and Matthew 15:10-20.

> Guard your heart above all else, for it is the source of life. —Prov. 4:23

> Summoning the crowd, He told them, "Listen and understand: It's not what goes into the mouth that defiles a man, but what comes out of the mouth, this defiles a man." Then the disciples came up and told Him, "Do You know that the Pharisees took offense when they heard this statement?" He replied, "Every plant that My heavenly Father didn't plant will be uprooted. Leave them alone! They are blind guides. And if the blind guide the blind, both will fall into a pit." Then Peter replied to Him, "Explain this parable to us." "Are even you still lacking in understanding?" He asked. "Don't you realize that whatever goes into the mouth passes into the stomach and is eliminated? But what comes out of the mouth comes from the heart, and this defiles a man. For from the heart come evil thoughts, murders, adulteries, sexual immoralities, thefts, false testimonies, blasphemies. These are the things that defile a man, but eating with unwashed hands does not defile a man." —Matt. 15:10-20

What do these verses communicate about the relationship between heart and behavior?

What are some ways our culture tries to influence change in behavior without turning to the heart (Elf on the shelf, etc.)?

In what ways does an emphasis on a heart change go against a works-based view of religion?

THE AFTERLIFE

What comes to mind when you think of eternal life? Heaven? Streets of Gold? Jesus helps us have a clear understanding of eternal life when he says, "This is eternal life: that they may know You, the only true God, and the One You have sent—Jesus Christ" (John 17:3). Sure, we can say that we will be with God in heaven one day, but that isn't the essence of eternal life. Eternal life is knowing Christ, communing with Him, and enjoying an ongoing relationship with Him. He is eternal life itself!

> After hearing John 17:3, does this change your perspective on eternal life? If so, how?

> How would you explain eternal life to someone now that you have this new perspective?

> Discuss how it belittles Christ when we reduce Him to being a mere ticket who gives us access to heaven.

A NEW ANALOGY

I once heard an analogy of world religions that compared them to a maze as opposed to a mountain with various paths. Unlike the mountain analogy, where there are many paths that reach the top, with a maze there is only one path that leads to the center. Sure, there are other paths throughout the maze, but these paths lead to dead ends. And like a maze, there are often paths that run parallel to each other for a given length of time, which is akin to there being certain points of commonality between differing religions like the sanctity of human life, the existence of an afterlife, etc., even though these parallel paths eventually diverge. There is only one true path, one that makes it past all of the dead ends and finally emerges as the sole way of truth to the center. And in a completely non-arrogant way, we have all reason and evidence to believe that true way is found in Christ Himself, who is "the way, the truth, and the life" (John 14:6).

TRUE STORY

I got a part-time job working at the local mall during my senior year of high school. Near the kiosk where I worked in was another small kiosk owned and operated by two brothers. Not too long after moving in I introduced myself to them. We often chatted on account that the mall could be pretty slow moving at times. After a while, the topic of religion came up in our conversations. I learned that they were both Muslim, and they learned that I was a Christian. From then on, the topic of religion came up pretty frequently.

The conversations we had over our religious beliefs were cordial. I asked one of the brothers a lot of questions regarding his beliefs and why he believed them, and he was able to do the same for me. I learned early on that although he is a Muslim, he didn't believe himself to be a very good one. He admitted to not being committed or following through with the Five Pillars of Islam, especially when it came to prayer, fasting, and making the pilgrimage to Mecca. Because of his lack of works in these areas, he admitted to not having assurance of what awaited him in the afterlife.

Over the course of my time there I had many conversations with him, discussing topics like who Jesus is, how we are made right with God, whether salvation can be earned, as well as the credibility of the Bible versus that of the Koran. I was still young in my own faith at the time and maybe didn't have all the answers he needed to hear, but just engaging in the conversations allowed me to be strengthened in my own beliefs and grow in my ability to communicate those beliefs to others.

DEVO

DAY 1

WHAT'S THE DIFFERENCE?

But there were also false prophets among the people, just as there will be false teachers among you. They will secretly bring in destructive heresies, even denying the Master who bought them, and will bring swift destruction on themselves. Many will follow their unrestrained ways, and the way of truth will be blasphemed because of them. They will exploit you in their greed with deceptive words. Their condemnation, pronounced long ago, is not idle, and their destruction does not sleep.

—2 Pet. 2:1-3

Years ago I taught a junior high school class on world religions. As the students and I walked through several religions and the beliefs they held, it became clearer and clearer to us that these religions all had certain things in common as well as certain points where they departed from biblical Christianity. Not only that, but it just so happened that these points of departure centered around Christianity's five nonnegotiable doctrines or beliefs—the person and nature of God (the Trinity), the person and work of Jesus (the fact that He is both fully human and fully divine), the sinfulness of humanity, salvation by grace through faith (as opposed to works), and the authority of the Bible. There are certainly other doctrines we could discuss that are important to the Christian faith, but overall, theologians have singled out these as being the historic pillars of what it means to be an orthodox Christian.

By the end of the course, students were able to evaluate the different belief systems and examine how each compromised on these five areas of Christian doctrine. They were able to see how all of the world religions were works-based while Christianity is grace-based; how nearly all religions respected Jesus and even sought to adopt Him into their religion even though they denied His deity; and how other religions trusted in sources of authority (their writings) and rejected the authority of God's revelation revealed in Scripture even though the Bible has been overwhelmingly proven to be more historically reliable and trustworthy in its accounts. And because students today are exposed to different religious beliefs on a massive scale, I would have students message me even years later to share how the class helped them sift through the different religious beliefs they encountered on their college campuses.

But before jumping in and studying what different religions have to say, it is important to first and foremost be grounded in the truth. It is similar to when I was looking to buy my wife a nice pearl necklace years ago—I had to do the research into the nature, look, and texture of what real pearls were like in order to be able to spot the fake ones people were offering me. If I had gone into my search not knowing what to look for, then I could have easily been taken advantage of and my wife, not to mention my wallet, would have suffered as a result.

How can you know if something you believe comes from God or from human philosophy?

STANDARDIZED TESTING

I mentioned previously that I taught a junior high school class on world religions years ago. And while the students learned to evaluate and critique other religious systems through a biblical lens, they also learned to evaluate those religions by just using helpful critical thinking skills as well. Utilizing these skills, students were once again equipped to weigh the merits of the various world religions they encountered. Here are the ones I suggested they master.

The test of reason: In other words, how do these different worldviews hold up to simple logical scrutiny? Do they contain any logical contradictions? One example of this can be seen in evaluating a claim like skepticism. Some skeptics claim that no one can know anything. Now, just by glancing at that claim it should be easily noticeable that there is a contradiction present. If one claims that no one can know anything, what reasons and support would we have to believe that claim is true? After all, the person just said no one can know anything, which must include that claim as well. There are several worldviews that fail this test of reason due to the logical contradiction within their system—Buddhism being one.

The test of outer experience: Worldviews also must be able to account for what we know about the world around us. If a worldview believes that pain and death are illusions, or that a lightning strike is the result of Thor banging his hammer and not the result of electrons and protons in the cloud, then we would do well to ignore them on the basis that they do not fit with what we know to be true about the physical world around us.

The test of inner experience: Just as with the world around us, worldviews should be able to shed light on what we know to be true about ourselves. For this test, what does the worldview have to say in regard to why we are unique from the rest of creation, why we are conscious to moral beliefs of right and wrong, why we feel guilt, and so forth? Worldviews that ignore or fail to adequately account for what we intuitively know about ourselves should be ignored.

The test of practice: While worldviews should be able to pass the "thought" tests above, they should ultimately be livable in the long run. Thus, for worldviews like Islam and Buddhism that have an impossible list of do's and don'ts to live by, red flags should emerge. For a religious belief to be true, it should be livable as well.

These are just some of the tests, among others, that people could use in evaluating the truthfulness of a religious worldview. Passing these tests, of course, doesn't necessarily mean that the worldview is true—other things would have to be considered as well. However, it does provide us with some initial tests that, in the end, can eliminate worldviews right off the bat.

> What can you do, starting today, to make sure you are never deceived and led away from the truth of Christ?

Dear friends, do not believe every spirit, but test the spirits to determine if they are from God, because many false prophets have gone out into the world.

This is how you know the Spirit of God: Every spirit who confesses that Jesus Christ has come in the flesh is from God. But every spirit who does not confess Jesus is not from God. This is the spirit of the antichrist; you have heard that he is coming, and he is already in the world now.
—1 John 4:1-3

Jesus told him, "I am the way, the truth, and the life. No one comes to the Father except through Me.
—**John 14:6**

JESUS IS UNIQUE BECAUSE OF WHO HE IS

What comes to mind when you hear the word "unique"? Perhaps you think about a unique piece of jewelry or a unique fashion trend, or maybe a unique talent or skill. By definition, in order for something to be unique it must stand out in some way. It must be superior or one of a kind.

In John's Gospel we see perhaps the greatest statement regarding the uniqueness of who Jesus is when we read that He is "the way, the truth, and the life." Each of these metaphors used to describe Jesus not only distinguishes Him from other religious leaders, but carries with it tremendous implications for us personally.

The fact that Jesus is "the way" and not just "a way" or even "the best way" teaches us a lot about how we are to relate to God. Years before Jesus was born, the prophet Isaiah warned the people of their waywardness by saying that, "We all went astray like sheep; we all have turned to our own way" (Isa. 53:6). Much like Adam and Eve in the garden, people throughout the centuries have been turning to their "own way" and have ignored the Bible's warning that when you do this, the path will eventually lead to death. "There is a way that seems right to a man, but its end is the way to death" (Prov. 14:12).

As mentioned in this session's video, the majority of religions recognize that something is not quite right with the world. They recognize that the world, as well as the people in it, is broken and in need of being fixed. The solution other religions provide, however, couldn't be further from the truth. For them, fixing the problem comes by means of self-improvement or doing good works, thinking that through such acts people can earn God's favor.

Christianity, however, has a very unique take on the matter given that Jesus is the single and unique way to God. Christianity believes that the path to God is not a list of "do's and don'ts," but rather a Person. It has seen what happens when people try to go their own way as in the case of Adam and Eve in the garden, and as a result teaches that no amount of effort or good works can restore our relationship with God apart from the Way God has provided.

Why do you think some people might prefer a list of things to do in order to get to heaven? Does this describe you? Why or why not?

JESUS IS UNIQUE BECAUSE OF WHAT HE SAYS

We live in a day and age that promotes the idea that all religious beliefs are true and valid. There are people across the cultural spectrum that hold to this idea of religious relativism, even in spite of the obvious logical contradictions this position entails. (After all, how can the belief that there are many gods and the belief that there is one God both be true at the same time?) In fact, religious relativism is so ingrained in our culture that to disagree with it will almost guarantee you the label of being religiously intolerant.

Of course, those who argue that people are being intolerant if they don't accept the validity of all religious beliefs have clearly confused these ideas. To be tolerant means to accept the idea that not everyone will believe as you do and that people can coexist with different religious beliefs. Thus, one can be tolerant of other religious beliefs without believing that all religious beliefs are true and valid. In fact, to see the inconsistency of the way the term is used, just look at the relativist who is intolerant of those who make exclusive religious claims like Christianity.

Religious relativism is nothing new to our culture—it has existed in various forms throughout the centuries. The first-century Christians had to face it in their own day, and as a result were persecuted to the point of death. Because they believed Jesus when He said, "No one comes to the Father except through me," they rejected the notion that Jesus was just one truth among many about God. They boldly proclaimed to those around them that, "There is salvation in no one else, for there is no other name under heaven given to people, and we must be saved by it" (Acts 4:12).

> Where do you see issues of acceptance and tolerance at school? in the media? Is your view of tolerance more similar to the world's view or the biblical view?

Jesus told him, "I am the way, the truth, and the life. No one comes to the Father except through Me.
—John 14:6

JESUS IS UNIQUE BECAUSE OF WHAT HE GIVES

Jesus told him, "I am the way, the truth, and the life. No one comes to the Father except through Me.

—John 14:6

Another thing that sets Jesus apart from other religious leaders is the new life that He gives. Jesus says, "I am the resurrection and the life. The one who believes in Me, even if he dies, will live. Everyone who lives and believes in Me will never die—ever" (John 11:25-26). No other religious figure claims to have the ability to raise the dead, nor has any other religious figure experienced a personal resurrection from the dead like Jesus. The fact of Jesus' resurrection makes Him, without a doubt, the most unique religious figure of all, highlighting the fact that He alone is not only the author of life, but that He conquered death by sacrificing His life on the cross so that we might have eternal life.

The resurrection is central to Christianity. If it didn't take place, Christianity would, as the apostle Paul said to the Corinthians, be a complete deception. Of course, the apostle Paul could say that because he saw, along with more than 500 other eyewitnesses, the resurrected Christ. But what other evidence is there to suggest that the resurrection actually took place? Why has the resurrection been so hard for skeptics to discredit, and why is it the best explanation of the historic facts?

» The resurrection fulfills prophecies from the Old Testament. (See Ps. 16:9-11; 49:15; 86:13; Isa. 25:8; 53:9.)

» Archaeological discoveries show that Luke made no mistakes in the geographic details of his writing. Luke indicates the resurrection as being the most important part of his Gospel.

» The first eyewitnesses to the resurrection were women. This is important because in the first century, women were not considered to be reliable witnesses. Thus, if the followers of Jesus were fabricating a myth about the resurrection, they would have said men were the first witnesses rather than women.

» The stone sealing the tomb probably weighed over 2,000 pounds and could only be moved from the outside. If the soldiers were asleep when the body disappeared (as they claimed to be in the Gospels), how could they know the disciples stole the body?

» The disciples were cowards who had abandoned Jesus during His greatest need. In addition, the fact that they would later demonstrate courage, even to the point of extreme persecution and death, would strongly suggest that they genuinely believed the resurrection of Jesus was true.

» More than 500 people saw Jesus after He rose from the dead.

The list of evidences for a historic resurrection can go on and on, all pointing to one inescapable conclusion: Jesus is Lord. Anyone who trusts in Him has the promise that they, too, can have eternal life.

What are some of your hopes and dreams for the future? When you come to the end of your life, what is your hope? Why is hope lost if the resurrection is not real?

HOW TO LIVE IN A RELIGIOUSLY DIVERSE WORLD

When I was in college I had the opportunity to visit a refugee camp. Hundreds of people from various countries and representing different religions were living in tents with very few belongings and in less than ideal conditions. While the camps do provide shelter, food, and medical care, they do not offer the comforts and familiarity of one's own home. Just a few years ago there were over 10.4 million refugees still displaced from their homeland, according to a past report from a UN Refugee Agency.[1] Those numbers have grown astronomically in the past two years.

While the people living in the refugee camps fled their homes due to extreme violence, I couldn't help but contemplate the religious diversity represented in these camps. People from all ends of the religious spectrum were present, and as a result I was overwhelmed at the thought that many of them may never have a faithful Christian witness in their lives or even hear the name of Christ.

My experience and the emotions I felt were not unique—others have experienced similar thoughts and feelings while being on a mission trip. However, it is amazing how a burden for the lost, how a passion for missions, can be so easily drowned out once the busyness in our lives takes over or the overload of entertainment from our culture causes us to forget. After all, out of sight out of mind.

In the end, a study on other religions should drive us closer to the biblical truth that from the beginning God set out a plan to redeem the entire human race. Though He used the Jewish nation as the means by which He would bring the Savior into the world, His plan always included the opportunity for every people group to know His Son. We are told in Revelation 7:9 that heaven will be filled with people from every tribe, nation, and language, no doubt the majority of whom were involved or a part of another religion before repenting of their sins and trusting in Jesus alone for salvation. God loves all people and desires they come to know Christ, and because of that we, too, should reach out to those in other religions by lovingly sharing the truth of the gospel with them. After all, we wouldn't be where we are now had it not been for someone loving us enough to tell us about Jesus.

What prevents you from talking to people who don't share the same background or beliefs as you? How might we approach people differently if we saw them through the eyes of Jesus?

When Jesus left there, He withdrew to the area of Tyre and Sidon. Just then a Canaanite woman from that region came and kept crying out, "Have mercy on me, Lord, Son of David! My daughter is cruelly tormented by a demon."

Yet He did not say a word to her. So His disciples approached Him and urged Him, "Send her away because she cries out after us."

He replied, "I was sent only to the lost sheep of the house of Israel."

But she came, knelt before Him, and said, "Lord, help me!"

He answered, "It isn't right to take the children's bread and throw it to their dogs."

"Yes, Lord," she said, "yet even the dogs eat the crumbs that fall from their masters' table!"

Then Jesus replied to her, "Woman, your faith is great. Let it be done for you as you want." And from that moment her daughter was cured.

—Matt. 15:21-28

Because of the day and age we live in, we are well familiar with the fact that other religions exist and that these religions make claims that are contradictory to the Christian faith. Our culture responds to this reality by simply lumping all religions into one category, thinking that they are all pretty much the same and, therefore, equally valid. However, it is clear that while religions share a lot in common, Christianity is a standout among them for several reasons.

AS YOU BEGIN TODAY'S STUDY, KEEP IN MIND THE FOLLOWING TAKEAWAYS FROM SESSION FOUR:

» Christianity, unlike other religions, is founded on historical evidences and reasons.

» Christianity is testable, unlike other religions.

» Christianity makes more sense both of our world and of ourselves than other religions.

» Christianity is grace-based versus other religions that are works-based.

» The biggest distinction between Christianity and other religions is the person and work of Jesus.

The world is full of people who believe in God's existence but have no awareness of how to be in right relationship with Him. Even though this session showed how distinct Christianity is among all religions, it should inspire and encourage us in the end to be on mission with God in spreading the truth of His gospel to the nations.

After having looked at how Christianity is unique and distinct among the religions, we now turn to another pressing question: Why is there evil and suffering in the world?

WHY IS THERE EVIL AND SUFFERING IN THE WORLD?

START

》》

SET THE SCENE

It's a typical weekday morning when you hear the news reports that another massive terrorist attack has taken place in our country. The details from the media begin to pour in as reporters recount the dozens of innocent victims that have tragically lost their lives to the senseless acts of extreme violence. Men, women, and children all brutally gunned down, the innocent targets of people wanting to commit acts of evil and cause suffering. In one of the reports, you hear an interviewee, overcome by the horrific evil of these acts, ask, "If God exists, why did he allow this to take place? Why didn't he intervene?" The question resonates with you, and you begin to think how you would respond. What would you say to that person?

WATCH

FROM THE INTERVIEW

For most people, suffering and evil is not an _____ problem.

For most people, suffering and evil is an _____ problem.

Suffering is used by God to help bring people freely to a _____ of Himself and to eternal life.

The _____ can't really say that there is evil in the world.

If anyone could complain of the problem of innocent suffering, it would be _____ of _____.

IN YOUR OWN WORDS

Explain the difference between the intellectual problem of evil and the emotional problem of evil.

How would you explain to someone that there is no contradiction between God's existence and the existence of evil and suffering?

How would you counsel someone struggling with doubts because of some sort of suffering in his or her life?

NOTES

In this section write down any additional thoughts, comments, or questions related to the interview.

DISCUSS

====================================»

What are your initial thoughts about the interview for this session?

What are some instances of evil and suffering that you have witnessed (or even personally experienced)?

Have you ever struggled with belief in God because of the existence of evil and suffering? If so, explain why.

Atheists try to use the existence of pain, evil, and suffering as an argument to prove God doesn't exist. Do you think that's possible? Explain.

Why is it that atheists, who reject God, have no reason to believe in the existence of objective evil? How does their rejection of God actually hurt their argument?

Why is it important to make the distinction between the intellectual problem of evil and the emotional problem of evil?

Why is the existence of God and the existence of evil not logically incompatible?

What might be some good reasons for God to allow evil and suffering to take place in our world?

When it comes to answering questions related to the topic of evil and suffering, it's important to recognize the true nature behind what's being asked. Consider the following examples:

» If God created a good world without sin, where did evil come from?

» Why did God allow my mom to die from cancer?

» Where was God during 9-11? Why didn't He stop the terrorists?

» If God loves me, why would I being going through so much pain over this broken relationship?

Which questions do you think are intellectual, emotional, or both?

What are some possible responses to questions like these?

DO WE SUFFER BECAUSE OF BECAUSE WE LACK FAITH?

There are some who would like us to believe that pain and suffering in our lives is the direct result of a lack of faith. "If only we had more faith," they claim, "would we experience the health, wealth, and prosperity in our lives that God desires."

Read Hebrews 11:1-34.

What is the common denominator shared between all of these heroes of the faith?

Were the things that happened to them because of their faith positive or negative? It is overwhelmingly positive, as seen in instances like crossing the Read Sea and the walls of Jericho falling, etc.

Read Hebrews 11:35-40.

What do the biblical heroes in these verses share in common with all of the others?

Why is it important to emphasize that every person mentioned in this chapter lived by faith despite whether they suffered or not? It is important because this chapter completely overturned the idea that bad things happen to us when we lack faith. Every person in this chapter lived "by faith"—both those who escaped the edge of the sword as well as those who died by the sword.

Not only does Hebrews 11 dispel the myth that suffering comes from a lack of faith, but also consider the sufferings of the apostle Paul himself. In 2 Corinthians, Paul recounts some of his sufferings because of his faith and commitment to Christ when he says:

> Five times I received 39 lashes from Jews. Three times I was beaten with rods by the Romans. Once I was stoned by my enemies. Three times I was shipwrecked. I have spent a night and a day in the open sea. On frequent journeys, I faced dangers from rivers, dangers from robbers, dangers from my own people, dangers from the Gentiles, dangers in the city, dangers in the open country, dangers on the sea, and dangers among false brothers; labor and hardship, many sleepless nights, hunger and thirst, often without food, cold, and lacking clothing.
>
> Not to mention other things, there is the daily pressure on me: my care for all the churches (2 Cor. 11:24-28).

Why do you think Paul endured a life of such hardships?

What role do you think his faith played in being able to endure such sufferings?

EVIL AND THE CROSS

In his book *No Easy Answers,* Dr. Craig tells the story of three men standing before God's throne on judgment day:

> Each had a score to settle with God. "I was hanged for a crime I didn't commit," complained one man bitterly. "I died from a disease that dragged on for months, leaving me broken in both body and spirit," said another. "My son was killed in the prime of his life when a drunk behind the wheel jumped the curb and ran him down," muttered the third. Each was angry and anxious to give God a piece of his mind. But when they reached the throne and saw their judge with His nail-scarred hands and feet and His wounded side, a "man of sorrows and acquainted with grief," each mouth was stopped.[1]

In other words, these men were silenced by the reality of the cross of Christ—the fact that Jesus, an innocent man, was abandoned by those closest to Him, arrested on trumped up charges, and unjustly sentenced to death in a way that is unimaginably brutal. His body, too, was broken, not only by the cross but also by lashings and beatings, and He, too, experienced inner conflict when the Father turned away as He bore our sins on the cross. Christ, who knew no sin, became sin on our behalf, so that in Him we might become the righteousness of God.

TRUE STORY

For the most part it was a typical Wednesday night youth gathering at the church. We were closing in on our walk-thru study of the Book of Genesis. I spoke. The praise band led worship. And there was plenty of time for socializing and fellowship among the student body.

At the end of our service, when everyone was preoccupied with either food or foosball, a student approached me with a serious look on her face. She had been visiting the church for a while by this point, coming with some friends who were committed members of the youth group. Having only spoken with her a few times, I wasn't quite sure what to expect. She began by talking about the lessons in Genesis we had recently covered, especially the ones regarding Joseph and how God had used the terrible things that had happened to him for his good in the end. I was encouraged by this news, especially since I was told by her friends in the group that she claimed to be agnostic in her beliefs about God.

The more she talked, the more I got the impression that she was holding something back. Given that most of her comments were about Joseph and the things he went through, I wondered if she might be wrestling with any particular pain or suffering in her own life. Without prying, I simply looked at her and said, "You know, I think we all know deep down that the world isn't the way it was supposed to be. And if that's the case, I wonder why we think that." Not knowing quite sure how that would land, I awaited her response. And from the tears welling up in her eyes, my suspicions were confirmed—she was struggling with the problem of evil in her world. After that, I was able to connect her with some godly women in our student ministry who would be able to go a little deeper into both the intellectual and emotional issues she was dealing with in response to the pain in her life.

Because everyone experiences suffering and the effects of evil on some level, having conversations over this topic can become a pretty frequent occurrence. Knowing what to say, and how to say it, is an invaluable tool in helping others navigate this big question that touches both the mind and the heart.

THE "WHO" IS GREATER THAN THE "WHY"

Then Job stood up, tore his robe, and shaved his head. He fell to the ground and worshiped, saying:

Naked I came from my mother's womb, and naked I will leave this life. The LORD gives, and the LORD takes away. Praise the name of Yahweh.

Throughout all this Job did not sin or blame God for anything.

—Job 1:20-22

The natural response to experiencing suffering is to ask the "why" question. "Why is this happening?" "Why did God allow this?" "Why me?" These are the same questions that have raced through the minds of countless people throughout the centuries.

While it is common for people to ask the "why" questions in times of suffering, the reality is that greater peace comes not by way of answering the "why" questions, but in answering the "who" question as in the case of Job. We know from the first two chapters that it was Satan who asked God for permission to bring suffering and affliction into Job's life. God allowed Satan to proceed, knowing that He would use these dark and difficult times to reveal more of Himself to Job.

While we know the back story of what was taking place, Job didn't. And yet the author of the book still affirms that what Job said was true when Job stated that his sufferings came from God. Even though Satan was the one behind these terrible disasters and tragedies in Job's life, both Job and the author recognized that God must have at least allowed them to take place given the fact that He is sovereign over all things and all people.

When we ask the "who" questions like Job did, we come face to face with the God who has sovereign control of all things and is working all things for the good of those who love Him and are called according to His purposes (Rom. 8:28). Whatever the source of our suffering might be, knowing that God is good and that He is sovereign brings the type of lasting comfort we are really looking for during difficult times. Satan wasn't free to do anything he pleased—he had a leash around his neck and could only go to the point that God allowed. All of suffering should be looked at the same way—it is being held back and used by God's infinite wisdom that not only works for our ultimate good and joy in the end, but also for His glory.

Is it easier to accept that God is in control when good things are happening to you? Do you find it more difficult to believe He is in control when bad things happen? Why or why not?

THERE IS MORE THAN ONE WAY TO SUFFER

When it comes to the issue of suffering, it's important to take a step back and see how the Bible distinguishes between the different kinds of suffering we might experience. For starters, the Bible often talks about the type of suffering that results from wrongdoing. This type of suffering comes as a consequence for doing what is evil and wrong. An example might be someone who has consistently abused his body with drugs for years and now suffers from organ failure as a result, or someone who has decided to rob a bank and is subsequently caught and sent to prison.

A second type of suffering found in the Bible is the persecution people experience for the sake of the gospel. This type of suffering doesn't come as a result of doing something morally wrong or evil, but quite the opposite—it occurs as a result of standing firm in Christian beliefs. Examples of this type of suffering have been recorded throughout the centuries by Christian martyrs and missionaries who have faced tremendous persecution as a result of their faith.

Finally, the Bible talks about the type of suffering that simply comes as a result of living in a fallen and broken world. Ever since sin entered the world through human rebellion, humanity has experienced the effects of this brokenness on a universal scale. People suffer as a result of natural disasters or famine, as well as just simply living in a world where bad things happen. It is the type of suffering that comes from unforeseeable and uncontrollable car accidents, or even the type of accidental suffering that might come from playing sports.

In the end, it is clear that not all suffering is the same, which is why it is helpful to look at all of the possible causes the Bible describes. This can shed light on the type of suffering someone might be experiencing, and can equip the person who is suffering to know how to respond. If someone is suffering as an evildoer, then the Bible is clear that they should repent of their sins and take refuge and comfort in God. If they are suffering for righteousness' sake, then their response should be one of joy and rejoicing, knowing that there is a special promise of blessing that comes with this type of suffering. If they are suffering for the simple reason of living in a broken and sinful world, then they should yield to the grace of God knowing that, as Paul did, His grace sufficient in our weakness (2 Cor. 12:9).

When you see or experience suffering, what is your first reaction? How will understanding suffering from this perspective affect how you view it and what you learn from it?

None of you, however, should suffer as a murderer, a thief, an evildoer, or a meddler.
—1 Pet. 4:15

Those who are persecuted for righteousness are blessed, for the kingdom of heaven is theirs.
—Matt. 5:10

At that time, some people came and reported to Him about the Galileans whose blood Pilate had mixed with their sacrifices. And He responded to them, "Do you think that these Galileans were more sinful than all Galileans because they suffered these things? No, I tell you; but unless you repent, you will all perish as well! Or those 18 that the tower in Siloam fell on and killed—do you think they were more sinful than all the people who live in Jerusalem? No, I tell you; but unless you repent, you will all perish as well!"
—Luke 13:1-5

PREPARING FOR THE INEVITABLE

Consider it a great joy, my brothers, whenever you experience various trials, knowing that the testing of your faith produces endurance. But endurance must do its complete work, so that you may be mature and complete, lacking nothing.

—Jas. 1:2-4

When I was in graduate school I used to have this recurring dream (or what felt more like a nightmare). In the dream I was taking a full load of classes. However, because of the workload and everything else, there was one class that I would always forget to attend. When I finally did show up to the class it was test day, and I had no clue how I was going to pass the test. It was a horrible dream that carried with it horrible feelings. In fact, I used to wake up feeling completely anxious and overwhelmed until I realized it was just a dream.

I realize that this may sound like something that's not worth getting upset over. But I was working hard in school, and making good grades was important to me. The thought of missing several classes and showing up on test day completely unprepared made me sick to my stomach. Not only would a failing grade be a waste of the money I was spending on my education, but it would highlight my own laziness and procrastination in my school work.

I often think about the idea of having to take a test when it comes to the issue of suffering. Taking tests are a natural part of life, much like suffering. Whether we want to take them or not, or whether or not we feel prepared to pass them, tests continue to come our way. Suffering is much the same way.

Like tests, suffering is inevitable. Everyone will experience suffering to some degree or another in this life. No one is immune or gets a free pass. However, what we can do is prepare our hearts and souls for when those times come. We can fix our eyes on Jesus and ground ourselves in God's Word to the point that when suffering does come our way, we don't lose our joy in Him because of the circumstances of our suffering. Even if we can't prevent them from happening, we can prevent them from derailing us spiritually. And when we respond in this way, we come to realize that like tests, moments of suffering are just a small part of a much larger class we are taking. When suffering is viewed in its proper perspective, we have the advantage of seeing how in the end suffering can contribute positively to the overall class of life each of us are enrolled in.

What is the most difficult situation you have ever experienced? Where did you find hope in the midst of your struggle? What makes it difficult for you to trust God in your struggles?

CAN ANY GOOD COME FROM SUFFERING?

It's hard to imagine while going through a season of suffering that it could somehow be used for our good and joy in the long run. The pain can be so intense that we can't see past our immediate circumstances, causing us to be blind to the light God can eventually shine into our darkest moments. Like a mosaic composed of a thousand individual tiles revealing a much larger picture, we are standing so close to our suffering that we are incapable of stepping back and seeing how all these things might be used to shed light on the work God is doing in our lives.

Because of moments like these, we need to look to God's Word to understand how He can use suffering in our lives for both His glory and our good and joy. We need to hear the story of Joseph and how God used the evil that was done to him at the hands of his brothers to save an entire generation of people (Gen. 50:20). We need to be encouraged by the fact that times of personal growth and refinement of character often come through moments of suffering rather than moments of laughter (Eccl. 7:3-4). We need to follow Paul's lead and cling to the grace and mercy of God, recognizing our complete dependence upon Him as we draw comfort from the fact that He sustains us during our weakest moments (2 Cor. 12:9). And as we go through the Bible and learn how the tapestry of suffering has been used to shape and mold and refine the hearts of other believers, we can walk away assured that in the end God knows what He is doing. He knows exactly what it will take to make us more like His Son.

As C. S. Lewis once said, "Pain insists upon being attended to. God whispers to us in our pleasures, speaks in our consciences, but shouts in our pains. It is his megaphone to rouse a deaf world."[2] While pain and suffering aren't things that we necessarily go looking for, they aren't something that we necessarily run from at all costs either. God is good, and He is working all things—including our suffering—for our good and joy in Him.

When have you had a hard time understanding what God was doing in your life? Are you willing to trust "the God of all comfort" the next time you go through a time of suffering? Why or why not?

Praise the God and Father of our Lord Jesus Christ, the Father of mercies and the God of all comfort. He comforts us in all our affliction, so that we may be able to comfort those who are in any kind of affliction, through the comfort we ourselves receive from God. For as the sufferings of Christ overflow to us, so through Christ our comfort also overflows. If we are afflicted, it is for your comfort and salvation. If we are comforted, it is for your comfort, which is experienced in your endurance of the same sufferings that we suffer. And our hope for you is firm, because we know that as you share in the sufferings, so you will share in the comfort.

—2 Cor. 1:3-7

WHEN SUFFERING, LOOK TO JESUS

Therefore, since we also have such a large cloud of witnesses surrounding us, let us lay aside every weight and the sin that so easily ensnares us. Let us run with endurance the race that lies before us, keeping our eyes on Jesus, the source and perfecter of our faith, who for the joy that lay before Him endured a cross and despised the shame and has sat down at the right hand of God's throne.

For consider Him who endured such hostility from sinners against Himself, so that you won't grow weary and lose heart.
—Heb. 12:1-3

Back when I was in seminary, I served as a college minister at a nearby local church. The college group was made up of young adults from all walks of life, some in college and some not. I remember counseling with a number of students over the topic of loneliness. The majority of them were single at the time, and they struggled with the desire to be married. Even though they were surrounded by friends and were in a community of believers, at the end of the day many of these students experienced strong feelings of loneliness because of their desire to enter into a marriage relationship.

I wasn't immune to similar feelings myself, so I pointed them to the source of my own encouragement during these times—Jesus. God the Son knows all too well—even more than we do—what suffering and loneliness feels like. On the night Jesus was arrested on trumped up charges, his disciples—whom He lived and served and broke bread with for more than three years—completely abandoned Him. And not only did they run, but Peter completely denied even knowing Jesus when asked.

The fact that the Son of God suffered and experienced temptation is encouraging because it means that we don't serve a God who is completely distant and unable to sympathize with what we go through. As the author of Hebrews points says, "For we do not have a high priest who is unable to sympathize with our weaknesses, but one who in every respect has been tempted as we are, yet without sin" (Heb. 4:15 ESV). Because Jesus is intimately familiar with the sufferings and temptations you and I experience, we can look to Him and find comfort in the fact that He understands what we are going through. And not only that, but that He is also with us, giving us the necessary strength to persevere.

When has God's presence comforted you in the past? How was this different from the kind of comfort that comes from the presence of friends or family members?

SUFFERING WITH OTHERS

Did you know that one of the worst experiences a human can go through is being isolated from others? In fact, it has been argued that the worst punishment for prison inmates is being held in solitary confinement, meaning no social interaction with other people for weeks or months at a time. We are social beings, designed by God to be in community with other people. If we lean more toward being an introvert, we still need relationships, even if those relationships are few in number. To go without social interaction completely can actually have detrimental effects on our mental health. Studies have shown that it warps the mind to let it soak too long in solitude.

We are social beings intended to live in community with others. This was the way we were originally designed, and it is the way Christians are commanded to live. There are lot of "one another" passages in the New Testament, all referring to how Christians are to interact with one another. A couple of examples include Galatians 6:2, which says, "Carry one another's burdens; in this way you will fulfill the law of Christ" or Romans 12:15 where Paul says, "Rejoice with those who rejoice; weep with those who weep." In other words, Christians should not only be there for one another when times are good, but in difficult times as well.

Being with a friend or family member during a difficult time in their life can provide a tremendous source of strength and comfort. In fact, we don't even need to say anything—just our presence helps. Look at the case of Job and his friends. It could be argued that the greatest thing his friends did for him was just show up and sit quietly with him for days. Their presence alone was a type of communication that didn't need words. They were there, weeping with their friend, which serves as a good example for us when we have friends who need comforting.

What friends do you have that are going through difficult times? How can you comfort them as they walk through their struggles?

Now when Job's three friends — Eliphaz the Temanite, Bildad the Shuhite, and Zophar the Naamathite — heard about all this adversity that had happened to him, each of them came from his home. They met together to go and sympathize with him and comfort him. When they looked from a distance, they could barely recognize him. They wept aloud, and each man tore his robe and threw dust into the air and on his head. Then they sat on the ground with him seven days and nights, but no one spoke a word to him because they saw that his suffering was very intense.

—Job 2:11-13

No one is exempt from suffering or the effects of evil—we all experience them to some degree or another. As we have seen, atheists try to use the existence of evil as an argument for the non-existence of God. Not only is there no contradiction between God's existence and the existence of evil, but the atheist himself is in no place to argue. According to his worldview, objective goodness or evil doesn't even exist. If he truly believed in objective evil, then he would be led to the inevitable conclusion that there must be a supreme moral Lawgiver who is objectively good.

AS YOU BEGIN TODAY'S STUDY, KEEP IN MIND THE FOLLOWING TAKEAWAYS FROM SESSION FIVE:

» It is important to make the distinction between the intellectual problem of evil and the emotional problem of evil.

» Everyone concludes now that there isn't a logical contradiction between God and the existence of evil.

» God may allow evil and suffering to take place for good reasons.

» When it comes to pain, evil, and suffering, God is not distant but near to us.

» The cross of Jesus proves to us that God is not immune from our suffering, but rather loved us to the point that He would joyfully suffer on our behalf to bring us to Himself.

The topic of pain, evil, and suffering is one that hits home for many, causing them to doubt or question where God is in the midst of it all. Th previous session not only helps those struggling with the intellectual problem, but also points to Christ and God's Word for those struggling with the emotional problem as well.

After having dealt with the question of evil and suffering, we turn to our last question of how we can live apologetically in light of everything we have learned over the course of this study.

HOW CAN WE LIVE APOLOGETICALLY TODAY?

START

SET THE SCENE

You are enjoying a nice evening dinner with family at a local restaurant when the dinner conversation turns to the topic of what you plan to do after you graduate from high school. Almost instantly, questions begin to come from every direction, "Do you want to go to college?" "What do you want to study?" "What profession do you want to go into afterward?" Before you even get a chance to answer, a family member interjects by saying you should choose a major that leads to a high paying job. That's all that really matters. While the thought of being financially well-off is appealing, you wonder if choosing a profession for that reason alone is right. You wonder if there is more that goes into such a big decision. You consider whether your faith has anything to do with the matter. How do you respond?

WATCH

FROM THE INTERVIEW

Apologetics is a _____ to be used in the hands of every Christian in order to make much of Jesus.

Christians didn't think that learning to _____ well was part of being a _____.

Apologetics gives a person a _____, settled faith.

You will not base your life on things you take to be _____.

You will base your life on things you _____.

You don't have to _____ all the answers.

IN YOUR OWN WORDS

How would you explain the importance of loving God with all of one's being, including the mind?

What are some ways you can grow in your love for God in this area?

How has this session encouraged you to be more bold in your apologetic conversations with others?

NOTES

In this section write down any additional thoughts, comments, or questions related to the interview.

DISCUSS

Read Matthew 22:37.

> He said to him, "Love the Lord your God with all your heart, with all your soul, and with all your mind."

Why do you think Jesus emphasized that we should love God with our minds?

Why is it important for Christians not to neglect loving God with their minds?

What does loving God with your mind look like? What are some ways you can strive to do better in this area?

Read Romans 12:1-2.

> Therefore, brothers, by the mercies of God, I urge you to present your bodies as a living sacrifice, holy and pleasing to God; this is your spiritual worship. Do not be conformed to this age, but be transformed by the renewing of your mind, so that you may discern what is the good, pleasing, and perfect will of God.

What is the connection between worship and having a transformed mind?

What are the benefits of having a renewed mind?

What does it mean to not be conformed to this world?

What does it mean to know the will of God?

How does one receive a renewed mind?

According to the apostle Paul, one aspect of worship involves the renewal of our minds. Once our minds are renewed and we allow the Word of God to saturate our minds and shape and mold our worldview, we can develop the ability to think biblically about other worldviews and beliefs that come our way.

In addition, having a renewed mind helps us to live rightly before God (not being conformed to this world). In other words, it's not just about thinking rightly, but living rightly as well. This last point is important because sometimes our beliefs and actions don't line up. There are times that we say we believe something, but in fact we live very opposite of what we say we believe. Think about it this way:

STATED BELIEF +/- ACTUAL PRACTICE = ACTUAL BELIEF

Example:

» *Stated belief:* stealing is wrong

» *Actual practice:* copy a friend's homework assignment to avoid a grade penalty

» *Actual belief:* stealing is permissible in certain circumstances

Have you ever heard of Eleanor Boyer? Probably not, and that's okay. I don't imagine she would want people knowing her name anyhow. Ms. Boyer, age 72 at the time, made the headlines several years ago on account that she won the New Jersey lottery of $11.8 million dollars (about $8 million after taxes).

> What would you do if you won $8 million dollars? What do you think Ms. Boyer did?

If honest, most people would say they would keep a large portion of the winnings, perhaps giving some of it away to family and/or good causes that could benefit others. However, Ms. Boyer gave all of it away—every single dime—to places like her church, the local fire department, and other groups that served the town where she lived. "Why," you ask. In an article in *The New York Times*, Ms. Boyer stated that, "No new car, no vacation. My life is no different. I've given it up to God. I live in His presence and do His will, and I did that from the start."[1]

Ms. Boyer serves as a great example to living out our professed beliefs. She believed that God had always taken care of her, and that belief influenced every decision she made.

None of us live out something we are not convinced about. We look at the evidences, we hear the reasons, and after careful deliberation, we are all in. The same is true with life and apologetics. Apologetics helps us to see the reasons for why we believe what we believe, thus strengthening the faith and beliefs we have that then turn us toward a more consistent way of living.

CONVERSATIONAL APOLOGETICS

Remember that apologetics is a ministry to others as you seek to help remove any intellectual obstacles that may prevent someone from developing faith in Christ. It isn't about getting into arguments or winning debates; it is about making much of Jesus as we lovingly and graciously present Him to those around us.

Perhaps one of the best ways to begin practicing apologetics is by simply allowing it to seep into to everyday conversations. Look for opportunities to steer conversations, inviting (but not pressuring) people to explain why they believe what they believe, as well as opportunities to present your own reasons for the beliefs you have. If someone were to say in passing, "I can't believe people today are wanting to defund abortion groups," you could easily guide the conversation with a simple question like, "Why do you think that?" or "What led you to the conclusion that abortion is okay?"

Keep in mind that during conversations with others, you have a limited window of opportunity to speak up and ask questions—so be ready. Look for opportunities to learn more about the beliefs of the person you are speaking with. And when the time comes for you to present your own, be sure to keep in mind both what you say and how you say it—your tone is just as important as you words.

Always make it your goal to help people think through what they believe and why, and in turn allow yourself the opportunity to present why you believe what you believe as a Christian. By giving them the chance to speak, not only are you given credibility as a person who actually cares about them, but you are able to be in a better position of helping that person see any inconsistencies within their beliefs. Don't be overwhelmed with wondering whether you are going to say the wrong thing. Remain humble and kind to those you speak with. And take heart and gain confidence in knowing that the Christian worldview isn't the product of human invention, but is the revelation of God Himself.

Practicing apologetics can be difficult work, but that shouldn't come as a surprise. In essence, we are challenging people to think about their core beliefs, and at times, graciously telling them that they should abandon their worldview for the Christian worldview. That can be a lot for a person to take in. They have been living in their worldview for quite some time. Like a house they have lived in for decades, where they know every square inch and where everything has its place, we are suggesting that they relocate to a house and neighborhood to which they have no knowledge. Nobody likes to move and be uprooted from everything that is familiar to them, which is why the supernatural work of God in the hearts of people is necessary for genuine transformation to take place.

TRUE STORY

When I was in graduate school years ago, I worked at a fitness club just down the road from where I lived. During my time there I became friends with an older gentleman named Henry. Henry would come to the gym every day around the same time. We would frequently talk while he was exercising, and through those natural conversations I got to know Henry pretty well. Over time I learned a lot of general things about him—where he was from, his family life, and so forth—and personal beliefs as well, such as his beliefs about God, life after death, and salvation. Uncovering what Henry believed about these things was never awkward. We were just two people who respected each other simply having a conversation.

It was through these simple conversations with a friend that I was able to present my own beliefs, the reasons I held them, and why he should consider them as alternatives to his own. For instance, Henry wasn't a Christian. He held to a pluralism of sorts (all religions are valid), so I was able to present the reasons why what he believed was not only logically contradictory, but how it also ignored the evidence and where the evidence leads. Not only that, but I was also able to get him to think differently about his own view of moral relativism, and how objective morality points to a single, objective Lawgiver (God).

I had many of these conversations with Henry over the course of several years, and during several I was able to present the gospel to him without any sense of awkwardness on either end. While it was always my intention to remove any intellectual obstacles to faith that Henry had, it never felt superficial given that our conversations were based on genuine friendship. Of course, that isn't to say that having cold-turkey conversations on personal religious beliefs isn't helpful—they certainly can be if done the right way. However, for me and many other apologists I know, the easiest and perhaps most effective way is to do apologetics in the context of having conversations with people, especially those with whom the Lord has already put in your path.

So get started with those around you. Have those conversations. Ask the right questions. Be on mission with Jesus as you give a defense for why you believe what you believe.

THE TASK OF APOLOGETICS

For God who said, "Let light shine out of darkness," has shone in our hearts to give the light of the knowledge of God's glory in the face of Jesus Christ.

—2 Cor. 4:6

If you ever take a course in philosophy, one of the first things you will study is Plato's *Allegory of the Cave*. The philosopher Plato asks us to imagine a scenario in which a group of people have been chained and imprisoned in a cave from infancy, facing a big stone wall on which the only thing they can see are the random shadows that come across it as their captors occasionally walk behind them. Having never been spoken to or having actually seen their captors with their own eyes, they have no knowledge of anything beyond these occasional shadows.

Plato invites us to imagine what would happen if by some chance one of the prisoners were to break free from his chains. He would turn around and see, for the first time, things he had never known of before. He would first see a fire (which would explain how the flickering shadows were projected against the wall), then he would see a staircase and follow it outside of the cave. Now, imagine his surprise when he stepped out and saw sunlight for the first time, or the landscape around him. Such sight and knowledge would be, to say the least, earth shattering given that the only world he ever knew was nothing more than a cold and dark hole in the ground.

I mention Plato's cave analogy because it is a lot like the practice of apologetics. Like the prisoner who discovers that what he thought was true wasn't, we too have been delivered out of darkness into God's marvelous light (1 Pet. 2:9). Much like the prisoner, we too have seen the light, but the light we see is the light that comes from God's Son. And because this Son has changed our lives, we are called to deliver the good news of hope to those still trapped in darkness. With Jesus, we are commissioned to be on mission with Him in the task of setting the captives free (Luke 4:18), and one of the tools at our disposal in helping us accomplish this mission is the study of apologetics. By understanding and practicing apologetics, we open the blinds and allow the light of God's truth to rush in, helping to eliminate any intellectual obstacles that might prevent someone from believing in God.

Do you have to be a theologian to share or defend your belief in God? Why or why not? What do you need to know?

WHAT DOES APOLOGETICS HAVE TO DO WITH LIFE?

We live in a culture that compartmentalizes personal faith from everyday life. Sure, there are politicians who claim that their faith influences their decision making, but more often than not the culture at large treats faith (the sacred) as if it is something that should be kept private and separate from other aspects of life (the secular).

People who argue this way often turn to Thomas Jefferson and his beliefs about the separation of church and state. However, as historians have pointed out, Jefferson was merely saying that the federal government wouldn't interfere with matters of religion—the state would not identify with a particular religion or make the practice of that religion mandatory for its citizens. In other words, Jefferson was arguing for the freedom to practice religion, not that religious belief should be kept out of the public conversation.

Despite what some may say, biblical faith has never been intended to be seen as merely a private affair or something that falls into the category of opinion. The Christian faith, as we have seen, deals with facts and evidences, and these facts and evidences turn into reasons for why we believe what we believe. Not only that, but these reasons also inform the way we are to live in this world, influencing areas like the type of person one should date, the type of job one should pursue, how one should think about cultural debates like abortion, marriage, and the environment, and so forth. The Christian faith speaks into every area of life, and because of that, the Christian should never divorce faith from everything else.

Apologetics will help us to remember this important truth. It will help us to think and see how the theological rubber of our beliefs hits the road of everyday life.

> When have you been caught unprepared to defend your belief in God? Why do you think it is important for us to understand how to defend our faith?

All Scripture is inspired by God and is profitable for teaching, for rebuking, for correcting, for training in righteousness, so that the man of God may be complete, equipped for every good work.
—2 Tim. 3:16-17

APOLOGETIC CHECKLIST (PART 1)

...but honor the Messiah as Lord in your hearts. Always be ready to give a defense to anyone who asks you for a reason for the hope that is in you.

—1 Pet. 3:15

When having apologetic conversations with others, it is important to remember a few things:

First, know what you believe. This point may seem obvious, but it is worth mentioning. You can't articulate the reasons for why you believe something if you don't first know what you believe. This means that far from just studying a bunch of arguments from archeology or science, you need to be grounded in the content of your beliefs so that you will be better equipped to explain why you believe them.

Second, know how to best communicate your beliefs. This point gets closer to the reasons we offer for why we believe something, but also helps us consider the best possible means of communicating those reasons to others. In other words, know the person(s) you are talking to and try to deliver the reasons for your beliefs to them in the best way possible. This may mean using illustrations and examples (as I have tried to do throughout this study) to get your point across, or using logical arguments in the form of a syllogism for those friends of yours who process information better that way. Whatever the method of delivery (stories, analogies, logical arguments, etc.), the trick is to match it to the audience you have.

Finally, pay attention to your own character and tone while doing it. This last point is just as important as the others even though it often goes ignored. There is no question that however good you may be at pulling off the first two with success, if you come across as a jerk and are rude and condescending to the people you talk with, they will dismiss whatever good reasons you gave. Your character speaks volumes about who you are, especially if claiming to be a follower of Christ. Thus, if your tone with others is negative or if you come across as less than interested in what they have to say, then your efforts to live out apologetics will unfortunately be in vain.

Why is it important to know your audience when defending your faith? In what ways would it be helpful to know what other religions believe and how that compares to Christianity?

APOLOGETIC CHECKLIST (PART 2)

We have already looked at some things to keep in mind when practicing apologetics—things like knowing what you believe, how best to communicate those beliefs, and the manner and tone in which to communicate them. But what about the actual practice of apologetics? What are some helpful tips for when you find yourself in conversations where you have to defend what you believe about God? Here are a few things to keep in mind:

First, when talking with someone, don't forget to ask them questions (and lots of them!). There are many benefits to asking questions. For starters, since Christians often feel as if they need to be the primary speaker in apologetic conversations—after all, they are the ones trying to speak truth and remove obstacles for their hearers—asking questions to the person you are speaking with will keep you from talking too much.

Second, asking questions helps us to understand the beliefs of the person we are talking to. Questions help us gain information about their worldview, and that information can in turn be used to help us decide on how best to navigate the conversation with them.

Third, asking questions puts the person we are talking to in the position of defending their own beliefs and why they believe them. If a person claims they believe that everything in the universe is here by chance, you can follow up that claim by politely asking them how they came to that belief: What evidences or reasons led you to that conclusion? In doing so, you are putting what philosophers call the "burden of proof" on that individual, and they are responsible for defending their beliefs.

Fourth, asking questions allows people to think through their own beliefs and the reasons they hold them. This is extremely important because most people have never thought through their own reasons for believing what they do. By allowing people to thoughtfully consider the reasons they hold to certain beliefs, you are giving them the opportunity to see any contradictions or lack of evidence that may exist in their own thinking. Once that happens, you are in a better position to offer positive evidence for the truth of Christianity.

Asking questions is so important that it shouldn't be overlooked or minimized. In fact, to be a successful apologist you don't have to have all the answers and know all of the evidences that are available. You just have to ask questions.

What will you do this week to get to know students of other faiths/worldviews better? How might this prepare you to share your faith?

While He was praying in private and His disciples were with Him, He asked them, "Who do the crowds say that I am?"

They answered, "John the Baptist; others, Elijah; still others, that one of the ancient prophets has come back."

"But you," He asked them, "who do you say that I am?"

Peter answered, "God's Messiah!"

—Luke 9:18-20

REMEMBERING JESUS WHEN DOING APOLOGETICS

We destroy arguments and every lofty opinion raised against the knowledge of God, and take every thought captive to obey Christ.
> —2 Cor. 10:5 (ESV)

And you were dead in your trespasses and sins in which you previously walked according to the ways of this world, according to the ruler who exercises authority over the lower heavens, the spirit now working in the disobedient. We too all previously lived among them in our fleshly desires, carrying out the inclinations of our flesh and thoughts, and we were by nature children under wrath as the others were also. But God, who is rich in mercy, because of His great love that He had for us, made us alive with the Messiah even though we were dead in trespasses. You are saved by grace! Together with Christ Jesus He also raised us up and seated us in the heavens, so that in the coming ages He might display the immeasurable riches of His grace through His kindness to us in Christ Jesus. For you are saved by grace through faith, and this is not from yourselves; it is God's gift—not from works, so that no one can boast.
> —Eph. 2:1-9

In the very first session we discussed two main aspects to apologetics: one defensive and one offensive. Defensive apologetics involves defending the truth of Christianity from its critics, answering objections and raising counter-arguments to those critical of the faith. Offensive apologetics, on the other hand, involves offering arguments of our own in support of the truthfulness of the Christian worldview, showing how it is more reasonable to believe than not to believe. And as we have seen, when both of these aspects of apologetics work together in the life of the Christian, he or she is able to help remove the intellectual barriers against belief for those genuinely seeking answers.

When it comes to apologetics, it has been my experience that people often try to say too much too soon. I was like this myself when first learning the reasons behind my faith. I wanted to share these reasons and evidences with all of my skeptical friends and family members, and when opportunities arose for me to share, I imagine that many of them felt as if they were drinking from a fire hose—too much to digest in a small amount of time. I had to learn from experience that I didn't need to divulge every bit of my knowledge over these subjects in just one or two conversations, but that I could, as time went on, allow the conversation to continue so that the person I was speaking with could digest what I was saying (and so that I could give thought to what they were saying in exchange). Keeping in check my desire to cover everything in one conversation not only helped my relationship with the other person, but also benefited them in the long run.

However important the role of apologetics can play in helping others see things clearer, it is just as important to remember its limits. Apologetics cannot change a person's heart. Sure, it can be used by God to remove obstacles to faith, but it can't create saving faith in the heart of a person—only Jesus can do that. We can't argue people into the Christian faith (even though it is our job to be winsome and persuasive). However, we can answer people's questions and introduce them to the only One who is capable of transforming them from the inside out—Jesus.

Have you ever tried to argue with someone about your beliefs? In what ways do you need to change your approach when it comes to sharing your faith?

DON'T LOVE APOLOGETICS MORE THAN YOU LOVE JESUS

C. S. Lewis, perhaps the most influential Christian apologist of the 20th century, wrote a fictional work years ago titled *The Great Divorce*. It is a fascinating story that takes the reader on a narrative journey through both heaven and hell. The majority of the book follows the main character as he listens in on various conversations between those who are citizens of heaven (Spirits) and those who are residents of hell (ghosts). In one of these conversations there is a ghost—an artist before he died—who travels to heaven just for the chance to paint the beautiful landscapes. One of the Spirits comes to him and asks why he would prefer to paint the landscape rather than simply enjoying it and living in it. After all, isn't that what all of the classic art was intended to do while they were present on earth—point to and give glimpses of a grandeur beauty that was to come? Given that he was now there to enjoy the source of that beauty itself, why would he seek to waste time looking at a mere painting of it? After a while it becomes clear that the ghost is more interested in painting the beauty than in the beauty itself. (Disclaimer: Lewis wasn't arguing that people can actually travel from hell to heaven. Again, it is a fictional work intended to communicate some fundamental beliefs about the Christian worldview.)

> *Jesus answered, "If anyone loves Me, he will keep My word. My Father will love him, and We will come to him and make Our home with him.*
>
> *—John 14:23*

After reading through that years ago, it struck me that apologists have a similar danger before them in that it would be quite easy to fall more in love with the act of telling others about Christ and the truth of Christianity than with Christ Himself. Because apologetics is often about looking at the evidences and reasons for Christian belief and winsomely communicating those reasons to others, apologists run the risk of performing their craft to the neglect of developing their own relationship with God. Of course, that isn't to say that apologetics can't be tremendously beneficial to one's faith—certainly it can, as we have discussed already. However, it does take conscious effort to avoid falling victim to the mindset of loving the practice more than the One we are to tell others about.

Don't love apologetics more than Jesus, but rather let your love for Jesus overflow into a lifestyle of living apologetically. Apologetics is the means we use to communicate truths about Jesus and Christianity to others, not the end goal. The end goal is Jesus alone, and at the end of the day it is Jesus alone who will use our apologetic efforts to draw many to Himself.

What does your lifestyle currently communicate about your love for Jesus? What are some practical ways you can continue to grow in your faith so that you are always prepared to defend the truth?

We have learned a lot over the course of this study, having investigated and explored serious answers to some of life's most serious questions. While there have been points of application along the way, this last session looked more closely as to why we should do apologetics in the first place, as well as how we can live apologetically today.

TAKEAWAYS FROM SESSION SIX:

» Christians are commanded to love God with their entire being—mind included!

» Apologetics is a tool to help defend the faith, as well as a tool to help commend the faith to others.

» Apologetics is a ministry that seeks to remove intellectual obstacles to faith.

» Apologetics is a lifestyle and most naturally takes place through natural conversations with others.

» Apologetics isn't about knowing all the answers or winning every argument—it is about making much of Jesus as we seek to make Him known to the people we talk to.

LEADER GUIDE

START

==>>

As you prepare to lead this session, read through the following content ahead of time, highlighting any information you would like to focus on during the group time. Note that italicized content on these pages is not part of the student material but is specific to your role in helping facilitate group discussion.

To begin the session, lead students through the following scenario. Keep in mind that it is not necessary to identify right or wrong answers. The purpose is to get students thinking and discussing potential answers to common apologetic questions. We will revisit this scenario toward the close of the session.

SET THE SCENE

You and your best friend are studying together for an upcoming test. You notice that she isn't saying much—regarding school or anything else. You get a sense that something is troubling her, and after a little prompting she begins to explain how difficult life has been lately, especially when it comes to her faith in God. When you ask her what she means by that, she goes on to say that she's having all sorts of doubts about whether Christianity is true, whether the Bible is reliable, and whether Jesus is who He says He is, among other things. Not only that, but she starts to open up about some other difficulties in her home and social life, which makes you wonder what might be at the root of these struggles. Your friend looks directly at you with genuine sincerity and asks, "How can I know for sure my beliefs are true?" How do you respond?

WATCH

==>>

Direct students to use the video guide to follow along with the interview between Andy and Sean McDowell. Encourage them to fill in the blanks of the key statements, as well as write down additional notes on other important information in the space provided. Be sure to preview the session video ahead of time so you can develop your own notes to discuss during the group time. Note: Because this introductory video is a little longer than the rest of the videos in this series, be sure to plan your group time accordingly.

FROM THE INTERVIEW

Apologia – a verbal <u>defense</u>

Doubt is not necessarily a <u>bad</u> thing.

Our answers to big questions <u>shape</u> every decision that we make.

When people doubt, they tend to think it's only <u>intellectual</u>.

Identify the <u>source</u> of your doubts.

Doubt is not the <u>opposite</u> of faith.

Knowledge does not require <u>certainty</u>.

Christianity is based upon claims to <u>objective</u> truth.

DISCUSS

Lead students through the following questions. As you walk students through this element of the session, highlight content you want to focus on. Select students to read aloud the Scripture passages, and invite them to share any additional questions or comments.

Have you ever experienced doubt when it comes to your beliefs? If so, what are some of the doubts or questions you've wrestled with?

How did having these doubts make you feel? Why do you think most people feel ashamed for having doubts or asking questions?

Did you share these doubts with a trusted friend? If so, what was the end result? If not, why?

What are the dangers of trying to think through our doubts alone? *By not sharing our doubts with others, we may prevent ourselves from actually finding the answers we need. Other people who may know more about whatever it is we are struggling with could potentially help us if they knew of our doubts.*

How can avoiding the doubts we have hinder our ability to grow in our relationship with God? *If we avoid our doubts and end up constantly struggling with our faith, we run the risk of being ineffective witnesses for Christ. Not only that, but avoiding our doubts and never finding answers can cause us to shipwreck our own faith, eventually falling into unbelief.*

In what ways could facing our doubts and seeking answers for them make us stronger Christians? *By overcoming our doubts and finding biblical answers to our questions, we allow ourselves to be better grounded in truth, which in turn allows us to mature in our faith.*

What do you think causes us to doubt? Why is it important to think about where our doubts stem from (intellectual, moral, volitional)? *Identifying the source of our doubts will help us to not only understand where they are coming from, but also how best to address them. For instance, if our doubts are coming from some place of immorality in our lives, we should first own up to that reality and repent of our sins in order to address our doubts honestly.*

 WHAT DO I DO WITH MY DOUBTS?   **93**

FAITH AND DOUBT

Having doubts is a natural byproduct of our human nature—we are finite beings incapable of fully understanding an infinite God, even though we can know Him personally. There is a story of the church father St. Augustine who, during the writing of his important work on the Trinity, was walking down the Mediterranean beach in his homeland of North Africa when he came upon a small boy scooping the ocean water into his hands and pouring it over and over into a hole he had carved out of the sand. Augustine asked him what he was attempting to do, to which the boy replied that he was emptying the ocean into this small hole in the sand. Augustine asked, "How could such a vast body of water be contained in such a small hole?" And without delay the boy responded, "How could Augustine expect to contain the vast mystery of God in the mere words of a book?"

Like Augustine, we are finite creatures trying to talk about the infinite being who created all things. Our best attempts merely scratch the surface. However, even though doubts may arise due to our shortcomings, it doesn't mean that we can't know things within a reasonable degree of certainty, having full assurance that the beliefs we hold are, in fact, true and justified beliefs.

There are many within our culture, particularly atheists, who say that faith is blind and goes against reason. However, this description of faith is not the biblical portrait we see in Scripture. Faith in Scripture never goes against reason, and is certainly not a blind intellectual leap in the dark. Instead, the Bible always presents faith as reasonable belief, founded upon evidences and historical events that took place in time-space-history.

What is faith? Here is a good working definition: "Faith is fundamentally a relational matter; it is about trusting God. Yet part of the inner dynamic of the life of faith is a desire to understand more about who and what we trust."[1] As Anselm said centuries ago, it is a faith that seeks understanding.

When it comes to faith, there are three important ways the Bible describes what it means in the life of a Christian:

Faith as:

Trust: *One of the primary ways the Bible talks about faith has to do with simple trust and confidence in God. Because God's character is trustworthy and reliable, and because His Word is accurate and true, we can trust Him and the promises He has made throughout Scripture. Thus, far from being merely an emotional response, genuine faith rests on God, even in the midst of confusion and doubt.*

Understanding: *Both the Bible and church history talk of a faith that seeks understanding. As Paul talks about in Romans 12:1-2, one of the appropriate responses to biblical faith is the seeking to have one's mind renewed and transformed for the purpose of being able to discern the will of God. Thus, far from being a blind intellectual leap into the dark, genuine faith always seeks to grow deeper in understanding the things of God.*

Obedience: *The third way the Bible describes genuine faith is one of obedience—in the way one lives his or her life. Following from trusting in God and growing in one's understanding of Him, faith works its way out into the everyday decisions of life. In this sense, faith isn't a private affair that is tucked away in the corner of life, but is something that is manifested in the way a person thinks, lives, and treats those around him.*

According to the Bible, faith has never been something that goes against reason. Instead, the Bible always presents faith as reasonable belief, founded upon evidences and historical events that took place in time-space-history. This is why Christian apologists throughout the centuries have defended their faith against critics by pointing out the intellectual and historical arguments that support the truthfulness of Christianity.

WHAT ARE SOME WAYS WE CAN GO ABOUT STRENGTHENING OUR FAITH?

1. LOOK TO SCRIPTURE.

Read Romans 4:18-21.

> He believed, hoping against hope, so that he became the father of many nations according to what had been spoken: So will your descendants be. He considered his own body to be already dead (since he was about 100 years old) and also considered the deadness of Sarah's womb, without weakening in the faith. He did not waver in unbelief at God's promise but was strengthened in his faith and gave glory to God, because he was fully convinced that what He had promised He was also able to perform.

How was Abraham strengthened in his own faith? *Abraham was strengthened by believing the promises of God (i.e. God's Word).*

Why do you think this is God's primary means to strengthening one's faith? *God's Word is the ultimate reason and evidence we have to support our faith. When we cling to His Word, we cling to the very reason for why we believe what we believe.*

2. LOOK TO JESUS.

Read Hebrews 12:1-2.

> Therefore, since we also have such a large cloud of witnesses surrounding us, let us lay aside every weight and the sin that so easily ensnares us. Let us run with endurance the race that lies before us, keeping our eyes on Jesus, the source and perfecter of our faith, who for the joy that lay before Him endured a cross and despised the shame and has sat down at the right hand of God's throne.

How do these verses describe Jesus' relationship to our faith? *Jesus is described as being the source (or founder) of our faith, as well as the perfecter of our faith, meaning He will sustain our faith forever.*

Read John 1:45-46.

> Philip found Nathanael and told him, "We have found the One Moses wrote about in the Law (and so did the prophets): Jesus the son of Joseph, from Nazareth!" "Can anything good come out of Nazareth?" Nathanael asked him. "Come and see," Philip answered.

After having a personal encounter with Jesus, Philip couldn't help but point others to Him. *Instead of coming up with arguments to present to Nathanael, he knew that a personal encounter with Jesus would be more effective.*

3. LOOK TO PEOPLE AROUND YOU.

Read Hebrews 13:7.

> Remember your leaders who have spoken God's word to you. As you carefully observe the outcome of their lives, imitate their faith.

Who are some biblical heroes in your own life that you can look to for answers when struggling with doubt?

WRAP UP

Remind students of the opening scenario we discussed at the start of this session. Invite them to revisit their initial answers and consider whether or not they would respond differently as a result of this discussion.

Take a few minutes to allow students to summarize some of the biggest personal "takeaways" from the session. For a helpful summary and main ideas, see page 20.

Discuss responses to the True Story on the following page. Invite students to consider how a similar experience might play out in their own lives.

Encourage students to complete the devotions for Session 1.

Finally, borrowing from the apostle Paul, close with prayer by asking God to shine within our hearts "the light of the knowledge of God's glory in the face of Jesus Christ" as we face our doubts and any lingering questions we have (2 Cor. 4:6).

TRUE STORY

As I mentioned in the video, my own story with doubt began in college and continued into my early years of seminary. For a long time it seemed and felt like I would always be plagued with questions in some form or another. Even when I would get some mental peace over a question I was struggling with, another one would inevitably pop up in its place. As a result, I felt like I was on this never-ending roller coaster, full of dramatic dips and corkscrews that were not only intellectual, but emotional as well given the overwhelming sense of shame I experienced during those seasons.

It was a difficult time in my life to say the least. However, I did eventually make it out of that place, in large part through the use of apologetics. The more I grew in my understanding of the Christian worldview, the better I became at discovering the reasons I believed what I believed. In doing so, I was able to address the questions that I struggled with.

I would be remiss not to tell you what took place during this time when I finally did open up to close friends about the questions I was wresting with. I initially struggled with the notion to "come clean" not only because of the shame I was feeling, but also because I didn't want to cause them to doubt as well. However, I was both amazed and somewhat relieved that many of my friends had been experiencing similar struggles. In fact, some of them were dealing with the exact questions that were troubling my own heart, but they felt ashamed to open up and share with others.

I say all of this to encourage you to not only meet your doubts and questions head-on with the truth of the Christian worldview, but also to encourage you to take up this approach alongside other Christian friends. By doing so, not only are you setting yourself up for your own success in this battle, but you could quite possibly be the encouragement someone else needs. Answers you've learned along your journey may play a crucial role in helping a friend in his or her own struggle with doubt.

WHAT DO I DO WITH MY DOUBTS?   **97**

START

As you prepare to lead this session, read through the following content ahead of time, highlighting any information you would like to focus on during the group time. Note that italicized content on these pages is not part of the student material but is specific to your role in helping facilitate group discussion.

To begin the session, lead students through the following scenario. Keep in mind that it is not necessary to identify right or wrong answers. The purpose is to get students thinking and discussing potential answers to common apologetic questions. We will revisit this scenario toward the close of the session.

SET THE SCENE

As you're scrolling through your social media news feed, you come across a blog post written by a university professor that was shared by a friend of yours. You click on the post and quickly notice that the main argument throughout states that morality is relative—that there is no objective right or wrong—and those that claim otherwise are trying to impose their morality on others. You see that your friend has already left a comment in support of this position. How do you respond?

WATCH

Direct students to use the video guide to follow along with the interview between Andy and William Lane Craig. Encourage them to fill in the blanks of the key statements, as well as write down additional notes on other important information in the space provided. Be sure to preview the session video ahead of time so you can develop your own notes to discuss during the group time.

FROM THE INTERVIEW

Cosmological Argument

Step 1: Whatever begins to exist has a <u>cause.</u>

Step 2: The <u>universe</u> began to exist.

Step 3: Therefore, the universe has a <u>cause.</u>

Moral Argument

Step 1: If God does not <u>exist</u>, objective moral values and duties do not <u>exist.</u>

Step 2: But <u>objective</u> moral values and duties do exist.

Step 3: Therefore, God <u>exists.</u>

Argument from Fine-Tuning

> Step 1: The fine-tuning of the universe is due to either physical <u>necessity</u>, <u>chance</u>, or <u>design.</u>
>
> Step 2: It is not due to physical <u>necessity</u> or <u>chance.</u>
>
> Step 3: Therefore, it is due to <u>design.</u>

DISCUSS

Lead students through the following questions. As you walk students through this element of the session, highlight content you want to focus on. Select students to read aloud the Scripture passages, and invite them to share any additional questions or comments.

How would you sum up the cosmological argument in your own words?

Why is it important to point out that creation isn't eternal but had a beginning? *Since it is logically and scientifically impossible for something to come from nothing, the fact that the universe had a beginning serves as evidence that Someone brought it into being.*

If the world were just the product of natural forces, what implications would follow? *There would be no objective right or wrong—whatever happens just happens. Not only that, but there would be no objective meaning to life since there would be no life beyond the grave.*

If the world were the product of a personal creator (which is what the evidence points us to), what implications would follow?

Summarize the moral argument in your own words.

Why is it difficult for the atheist to argue that morality is relative? *In the first place, it means that there would be no objective right or wrong, a fact that seems to go against everything we know. If that is the case, then torture or rape or mass killings from terrorists are nothing more than neutral outcomes of living in a world that is indifferent to pain and suffering.*

Imagine yourself back in time—all the way back to the year 1944. You are in Nazi Germany, and WWII is in full force. While most of the death around you is the direct result of national military forces warring with one another, you discover that another battle, one that is internal, is waging war for the soul of Germany itself—the Holocaust. You witness mass killings firsthand of those society has deemed inferior and biologically unfit to reproduce. You see the brutality displayed in these attempted exterminations by means of gunfire, poisonous gas, and massive oven chambers. And as you try to reason with the people of the day that such atrocities are absolutely wrong and should be stopped, those same people come back to you and say, "No, these acts aren't wrong because the culture deems them to be morally permissive."

> In other words, even if all of Germany thought what they were doing was acceptable, or even the rest of the world for that matter, would that have made it right? Explain.

What are some other moral issues that are not relative to time or culture?

1. racism
2. slavery
3. human rights
4.
5.
6.

Objective morals exist because an objective Moral Lawgiver exists—God. "I the LORD speak the truth; I declare what is right" (Isa. 45:19).

Read Romans 12:9.

> Love must be without hypocrisy. Detest evil; cling to what is good.

> **According to this passage, what does the Bible say with regard to the existence of objective good and evil? What should our response be?**
> *Paul tells us to hate or abhor what is evil, meaning 1) there is objective evil in the world, and 2) we should hate it. Paul tells us to cling to that which is good, again showing that there is objective goodness in the world and that we should run to it while avoiding evil.*

FINE-TUNING ARGUMENTS

There are so many fine-tuning discoveries that have been made in recent years that it would be impossible to mention all of them here. Here are just two from the area of cosmology that completely do away with the notion that our universe is here by chance.

1. *Gravitational force constant* (large scale attractive force, holds people on planets and holds planets, stars, and galaxies together) If this is too weak, planets and stars cannot form; too strong, and stars burn up too quickly. As Dr. Craig mentions in the interview, if this were altered in less than 1 part in 10^{100}, life as we know it would not be possible.

2. *Cosmological constant* (which controls the expansion speed of the universe) This refers to the balance of the attractive force of gravity with a hypothesized repulsive force of space observable only at very large size scales. It must be very close to zero; that is, these two forces must be nearly perfectly balanced. To get the right balance, the cosmological constant must be fine-tuned to something like 1 part in 10^{120}. If it were just slightly more positive, the universe would fly apart; slightly negative, and the universe would collapse.

How big is a number like 1 in 10^{100}? Just in case you aren't aware, that is the number 10 with one hundred zeros following it. Mathematicians actually call this number googol.

So how long would it take for someone to count to one googol? Well, it would be impossible. Just to give you an idea on how big a number this is, think about this: even if you were counting by two's, it would take you...

» 5 days, 18 hours, 53 minutes, 20 seconds non stop to count to one million.

» 15 years, 308 days, 6 hours, 53 minutes, 20 seconds non stop to count to one billion.

» $1.58 * 10^{92}$ years (or $1.58 * 10^{89}$ millennium) non-stop to count to one googol.

Like I said, you couldn't. In fact, the number googol is so high that there isn't even that many atoms in the entire universe!

I once heard a story from a philosopher asking us to imagine a conversation between two scientists following a successful space shuttle launch to the moon. "When the first moon rocket took off from Cape Canaveral, two scientists stood watching it, side by side. One was a believer, the other an unbeliever. The believer said, "Isn't it wonderful that our rocket is going to hit the moon by chance?" The unbeliever objected, "What do you mean, chance? We put millions of man hours of design into that rocket." "Oh," said the believer, "you don't think chance is a good explanation for the rocket? Then why do you think it's a good explanation for the universe? There's much more design in a universe than a rocket. We can design a rocket, but we couldn't design a whole universe. I wonder who can?"[1]

Why do you think it is difficult for some people to admit what seems obvious—that there is design all around us, and therefore there must be a Designer? *Oftentimes people have a preconceived notion of what they think is true, and then they try to interpret the evidence to fit that conclusion; or if they simply don't want it to be true, they likewise suppress what is obvious.*

How might these arguments be helpful when conversing with those who are more scientific and/or philosophically minded?

What other arguments like these do you know of that could be used in talking with an unbeliever?

WRAP UP

Remind students of the opening scenario we discussed at the start of this session. Invite them to revisit their initial answers and consider whether or not they would respond differently as a result of this discussion.

Take a few minutes to allow students to summarize some of the biggest personal "takeaways" from the session. For a helpful summary and main ideas, see page 34.

Discuss responses to the True Story on the following page. Invite students to consider how a similar experience might play out in their own lives.

Encourage students to complete the devotions for Session 2.

Finally, close in prayer, asking God for opportunities to explain to others some of the reasons for the hope that we have in Christ.

TRUE STORY

During graduate school I worked at a local YMCA. Many of my year-round co-workers were college students from nearby universities, and many more would join us during the summer months before heading back to school. Among these was a new guy, a sophomore student in college we will call Daniel, who was joining us for the summer break before returning to school.

My first day on the job with Daniel was entertaining to say the least. Daniel wasn't shy to express his beliefs, nor was he unwilling to defend them at all costs. The topic of that day: Is morality relative?

Daniel began discussing with other co-workers, who happened to be Christians, the issue of whether the moral beliefs we hold are objective (true regardless of whether anyone believes/practices them or not) or whether they were more aligned with individual preferences (along the lines of individual tastes, like cookies-and-cream versus mint chocolate chip). If they are objective, then everyone, no matter the time or culture in which they live, is obligated to follow them. If the latter, then people can just make their own decision, or follow what culture deems appropriate, when it comes to whether or not they will adhere to any particular moral belief system. Daniel was of the opinion that it was the latter.

When I arrived at work that day, other co-workers introduced me to Daniel and simply stated, "You guys need to talk." After hearing the context of the discussion, and after listening to what Daniel had to say, I asked Daniel if he could think of any time in history or culture in which it would be deemed appropriate to rape someone or torture children for fun if the cultural context allowed. He quickly, though hesitantly, responded by saying no. "Well, what about the holocaust?" I asked. It was the cultural belief of Nazi Germany that they were helping the evolutionary process along by exterminating millions of people they deemed to be inferior. "Was that morally permissible?" Again, Daniel responded by saying absolutely not.

I gave other examples that Daniel responded to with a resounding "no," making it clear that he didn't actually believe that all morality was relative. He intuitively knew, with the rest of us, that there are things that are objectively wrong, not dependent upon personal preference or culture. And once I was able to establish this fact, I was able to easily move into a discussion with Daniel as to where this objective morality is found—namely, in the character of God Himself, the Moral Lawgiver.

START

===»

As you prepare to lead this session, read through the following content ahead of time, highlighting any information you would like to focus on during the group time. Note that italicized content on these pages is not part of the student material but is specific to your role in helping facilitate group discussion.

To begin the session, lead students through the following scenario. Keep in mind that it is not necessary to identify right or wrong answers. The purpose is to get students thinking and discussing potential answers to common apologetic questions. We will revisit this scenario toward the close of the session.

SET THE SCENE

You're working on a group project for science class on the origin of the universe. One of the group members, a classmate you don't know very well, makes the off-hand comment that Christians are ignorant for believing in God when it is obvious that natural causes are sufficient enough to account for the existence of the universe as we know it. How do you respond?

WATCH

===»

Direct students to use the video guide to follow along with the interview between Andy and J. P. Moreland. Encourage them to fill in the blanks of the key statements, as well as write down additional notes on other important information in the space provided. Be sure to preview the session video ahead of time so you can develop your own notes to discuss during the group time.

FROM THE INTERVIEW

Interaction between Christianity and science has not been a <u>war.</u>

Science has discovered that the universe is <u>precisely</u>, delicately balanced so that life could appear.

Information always comes from an <u>intelligent</u> <u>mind</u>.

It takes an <u>intelligent</u> <u>designer</u> to explain irreducible complexity.

Science itself provides overwhelming <u>support</u> for belief in God.

DISCUSS

Lead students through the following questions. As you walk students through this element of the session, highlight content you want to focus on. Select students to read aloud the Scripture passages, and invite them to share any additional questions or comments.

What comes to mind when you think about the relationship between science and religion?

How does your perception of this relationship match up to the way this discussion is often presented in culture?

Have you ever felt like you had to choose between science or your faith? If so, why?

What stood out to you the most during the video interview for this session? Explain.

In looking at the history of science, why is it important to note that the Christian worldview paved the way for the scientific enterprise? *It is important to point this out for the simple reason that science and Christianity are not at odds with each other. Anyone looking at the history of science will see that modern-day science was born out of the Christian worldview. Scientists such as Copernicus, Francis Bacon, Johannes Kepler, Galileo, Descartes, Pascal, Isaac Newton, Robert Boyle, Gregor Mendel, and William Thomson Kelvin, just to name a few, believed that a Christian worldview provided the very intellectual foundation for science given the Christian belief that an intelligent God designed and created an ordered universe that could be understood by human beings. Unlike other religions that imagined every storm or movement of a bush was the direct cause of a god of some sort, Christianity argued that there is only one God, and He created a rational, orderly world that can be intelligibly understood. Indeed, the very fact that the order and design of the universe can be rightly understood by our human faculties is an amazing thing—one that is best explained by the Christian worldview of people being created in the image of God.*

DESIGN IS ALL AROUND US

How is design seen in other fields of investigation?

SETI: *Search for Extraterrestrial Intelligence looks for encoded messages from natural phenomenon in outer space. If researchers were to hear the first 20 prime numbers in a row, for example, they would conclude that this is not part of the natural universe but the product of an intelligent mind.*

Detectives: *Much like scientists, detectives look at the evidence and develop hypotheses that lead to the best explanation.*

Archaeologists: *Archaeologists look for design during excavations and are capable of determining whether certain fragments or pieces are the product of an intelligent mind or the byproduct of nature.*

Insurance companies: *Insurance companies investigate suspicious claims, such as in the case of fires, to determine whether it was the result of arson.*

Cryptologists: *Cryptologists decipher whether a set of symbols is a secret message (design) or a random sequence.*

Discoveries from cosmology to biology reveal not only our universe, but how humans are so intricately designed that to believe it all happened by chance would require one to have way more faith than that of a Christian. Consider just a few fine-tuning conditions relating to just our planet.

1. If the earth were merely 1 percent closer to the sun, the oceans would vaporize, preventing the existence of life.

2. If our planet were just 2 percent farther from the sun, the oceans would freeze.

3. We must have a large moon with right planetary rotation (which stabilizes a planet's tilt and contributes to tides). In the case of Earth, the gravitational pull of its moon stabilizes the angle of its axis at a nearly constant 23.5 degrees. This ensures relatively temperate seasonal changes and the only climate in the solar system mild enough to sustain complex living organisms.

For the experts who are studying in these fields and following the evidence where it leads, what should they conclude about these findings?

Years ago there was a talk show host who would conduct interviews on the street, asking random people very basic questions. It was fun to laugh when people didn't know the answers, or when they would make up an answer that was incredibly ridiculous. On one episode, the host asked participants how Mt. Rushmore was formed (you know, the mountain that has the faces of four of our most popular presidents carved on the side). One participant responded with "erosion." Caught off-guard, the talk show host clarified, "Okay, you're telling me that the faces of four famous presidents were carved into the side of a mountain by the natural forces of wind and rain?" And with that, the interviewee responded with a resounding, "Yes!"

The comedy of this response is very similar to the claim that the universe we live in came into existence by chance. Like Mt. Rushmore, design is not only apparent, but the best explanation of the evidence that we have.

WHAT ABOUT EVOLUTION?

When it comes to evolution, here are some pointers to help you navigate the landscape. People naturally assume that the term "evolution" can only have one meaning, but that's far from true. Evolution can be broken down the following ways:

1. *Evolution:* This can broadly refer to merely change over time or any sequence of events in nature.

2. *Microevolution:* This refers to minor changes and variations within a species, such as the different finch beaks discovered on the Galapagos islands.

3. *Macroevolution:* Large-scale changes resulting in a new and distinct species.

   d. *natural selection*: the blind, undirected, and purposeless process that is believed to be sufficient in accounting for the origin and diversity of life

   e. *common descent*: the belief that all organisms have descended from a single common ancestor

   f. *random mutation*: the mechanism used by natural selection in determining which mutations and/or variations would give an advantage to a species, as well as which ones will not

Why is it important to define what one means by "evolution" in an apologetic conversation? *If people mean different things when using the term, they will often talk past one another without either side fully understanding the other viewpoint. Defining terms is always important.*

What scientific evidence is there to support the idea of microevoution? *Most textbook examples of evolution would fall under this category—finch beaks, the peppered moth, etc.*
macroevolution? *There is no purely scientific evidence.*

Macroevolution is driven more by worldview than by science and scientific discoveries. If someone with an atheistic worldview already accepts the belief that God doesn't exist, then he or she will assume that nature is self-sufficient in accounting for life as we know it. They will look at the evidence and try to interpret it to fit their preconceived beliefs about God. Thus, their conclusions are driven more from their theological beliefs than their scientific ones.

Science is not an enemy—it never has been nor is it today. Even atheist Stephen Jay Gould, widely regarded as America's greatest evolutionary biologist, was adamant that his own skepticism could not be derived from the sciences. He says:

> "To say it for all my colleagues and for the umpteenth million time… science simply cannot (by its legitimate methods) adjudicate the issue of God's possible superintendence of nature. We neither affirm nor deny it; we simply can't comment on it as scientists."[1]

Those who argue that science disproves God have gone beyond the bounds of legitimate science and instead are disguising their atheistic beliefs as science.

WHERE DOES JESUS FIT IN?

For hundreds of years, philosophers have wondered how everything holds together. What is at the essence of things? What is it that unites all things together? Speaking to philosophers at the Areopagus, the apostle Paul answered this question when he said:

> "Therefore, what you worship in ignorance, this I proclaim to you. The God who made the world and everything in it—He is Lord of heaven and earth and does not live in shrines made by hands. Neither is He served by human hands, as though He needed anything, since He Himself gives everyone life and breath and all things. From one man He has made every nationality to live over the whole earth and has determined their appointed times and the boundaries of where they live. He did this so they might seek God, and perhaps they might reach out and find Him, though He is not far from each one of us. For in Him we live and move and exist." —Acts 17:23-28

"In Him we live and move and exist." The answer to the age-old question of what unites all things and holds all things together, according to Paul, is Christ. All things were created through Him and for Him. We can investigate things like atoms and quarks, but in the end none of these things will make sense apart from the Creator.

WRAP UP

Remind students of the opening scenario we discussed at the start of this session. Invite them to revisit their initial answers and consider whether or not they would respond differently as a result of this discussion.

Take a few minutes to allow students to summarize some of the biggest personal "takeaways" from the session. For a helpful summary and main ideas, see page 48.

Discuss responses to the True Story on the following page. Invite students to consider how a similar experience might play out in their own lives.

Encourage students to complete the devotions for Session 3.

Finally, close with prayer, thanking God for making His glory evident in the things He has made.

TRUE STORY

Not too long ago I was speaking at a winter retreat for a high school student ministry. During the second day of the retreat, the youth pastor invited me to an informal "Question and Answer" time with the students. Having really enjoyed doing these in the past with other youth groups, I enthusiastically agreed to participate.

When the session started, the youth pastor opened the floor to anyone who had questions. As soon as the invitation was extended, hands went up all over the room. The first student who was called on asked a series of question having to do with science and faith, such as: "Does science contradict faith?" "What about evolution is true?" "What about the Big Bang?"

I was grateful for the student's questions and answered them one by one. Of course, this was certainly not the only time I have had the opportunity to discuss the relationship between science and faith. These opportunities come up frequently. However, I share this example with you simply to show how students today, your own peers, are wrestling with this very topic. They have questions, and to be quite honest, many of them feel as if they don't have anyone to turn to for answers.

What an encouragement it is to know that you can be the very help that many of your friends need when it comes to answering these types of questions. You can shed light on the history of science and Christianity, talk about the various and often misunderstood ways that evolution is talked about, or share with them the cutting-edge discoveries that point to an intelligent design within creation. And when the answers go beyond your own understanding, you can not only point them in the direction of helpful books and talks by some of the experts, but you can also come alongside of them in the attempt to find the answers together.

START

══════════════════════════════════════ ≫

As you prepare to lead this session, read through the following content ahead of time, highlighting any information you would like to focus on during the group time. Note that italicized content on these pages is not part of the student material but is specific to your role in helping facilitate group discussion.

To begin the session, lead students through the following scenario. Keep in mind that it is not necessary to identify right or wrong answers. The purpose is to get students thinking and discussing potential answers to common apologetic questions. We will revisit this scenario toward the close of the session.

SET THE SCENE

You and a friend are sitting at your house watching a late-night talk show. On this particular evening, one of the guest appearances happens to be a well-known politician who is running for re-election. The host begins to ask the guest about some of the different views and policies he holds, and one of the issues that comes up is religion. The politician responds by saying, "I'm more of a pluralist when it comes to religious belief, meaning I think all religions are pretty much the same when you think about it. Consider this analogy to explain what I mean: Imagine seeing an elephant and six blind men. The first blind man walks up to the elephant and grabs the tusk and says, "It is a spear!" The second feels the trunk and concludes, "It is a snake!" The third hugs the leg and says, "It is a tree!" The one touching the tail claims, "It is a rope!" Another feeling the ear states, "It is a fan!" And finally, the last blind man feels the elephant's side and concludes, "It is a wall!"

The politician goes on to express that religious beliefs can be viewed in much the same way. Each blind man, representing a different religion, only grasps a small bit of the big picture—of ultimate reality. They have a handle on it somewhat, and they do the best they can to describe it, but in the end, they are essentially talking about the same thing.

After hearing that, your friend turns to you and says, "That makes sense!" How do you respond?

WATCH

══════════════════════════════════════ ≫

Direct students to use the video guide to follow along with the interview between Andy and Craig Hazen. Encourage them to fill in the blanks of the key statements, as well as write down additional notes on other important information in the space provided. Be sure to preview the session video ahead of time so you can develop your own notes to discuss during the group time.

FROM THE INTERVIEW

The problem being solved in Christianity is the <u>sin</u> that separates human beings from God.

Salvation as a free gift from God is one of the <u>unique</u> features of Christianity.

Christianity isn't just a <u>religion</u> among all of the world religions. It's a unique <u>view</u> of the world.

Christianity is <u>testable</u>.

The <u>resurrection</u> of Jesus is one of the best-attested facts of the ancient world.

DISCUSS

≪ ══════════════════════════

Lead students through the following questions. As you walk students through this element of the session, highlight content you want to focus on. Select students to read aloud the Scripture passages, and invite them to share any additional questions or comments. .

What did you find interesting about the video interview?

What other religious beliefs have you been exposed to?

How have you thought about other religions in the past?

What do you think is the typical cultural attitude toward other world religions, especially as it is reflected in movies, music, and other art forms?

What does the existence of world religions tell us about ourselves?
The reality of various world religions is an interesting fact in itself. One of the things that it tells us is that humanity, unlike the rest of creation, is hardwired to worship, even if many don't know Who should be the object of their worship. It tells us that we all think that something is fundamentally wrong with both our world and us, which is why every religion tries to "solve" the problem of how things can be made right. However, only Christianity, and its notion of sin in the human heart, can accurately describe our situation and how things can be made right again.

THE UNIQUENESS OF JESUS

Jesus is often seen as a universal religious figure, meaning that numerous religions try to adopt Jesus and make Him one of their own. For instance, some Hindus think that Jesus might very well be an avatar of Vishnu, that is, a reincarnation of that particular Hindu deity. In fact, Gandhi, one of Hindu's most well-known teachers, believed that Jesus was one of the greatest religious teachers of all time.

 WHAT ABOUT OTHER WORLD RELIGIONS?   111

In Islam, Jesus is said to not only be a prophet like Muhammad, but also that He was born of a virgin, was a legitimate miracle worker, and that He will stand with Allah at the scales of justice at the end of time. In other words, he is a very prominent figure even among Muslims.

However, even though many religions appreciate Jesus and His teachings, it is clear that all of these religions fail to acknowledge the truth of who Jesus claimed to be—God in flesh. They appreciate Jesus' teachings on love and grace, but they completely ignore the rest of Scripture that talks about Jesus' identity as the incarnate Son of God who came to save and rescue us when we were completely unable to rescue ourselves. Yes, Jesus is loving, and He talked a great deal about what it means to love God and one's neighbor. But Jesus is also the One who will one day judge humanity and make all things right again.

What are some other religions that fail to acknowledge the truth of Jesus' person and work?

How does the resurrection demonstrate Jesus' uniqueness among the leaders of other religions?

WORKS VERSUS GRACE

Read Proverbs 4:23 and Matthew 15:10-20.

> Guard your heart above all else, for it is the source of life. —Prov. 4:23

> Summoning the crowd, He told them, "Listen and understand: It's not what goes into the mouth that defiles a man, but what comes out of the mouth, this defiles a man." Then the disciples came up and told Him, "Do You know that the Pharisees took offense when they heard this statement?" He replied, "Every plant that My heavenly Father didn't plant will be uprooted. Leave them alone! They are blind guides. And if the blind guide the blind, both will fall into a pit." Then Peter replied to Him, "Explain this parable to us." "Are even you still lacking in understanding?" He asked. "Don't you realize that whatever goes into the mouth passes into the stomach and is eliminated? But what comes out of the mouth comes from the heart, and this defiles a man. For from the heart come evil thoughts, murders, adulteries, sexual immoralities, thefts, false testimonies, blasphemies. These are the things that defile a man, but eating with unwashed hands does not defile a man." —Matt. 15:10-20

What do these verses communicate about the relationship between heart and behavior? *As mentioned in the interview, one of the big differences between Christianity and other world religions is the fact that Christianity focuses on an internal change (heart) that leads to external change (behavior), while other religions focus primarily on external change (behavior) alone.*

Even in our own culture, we see a focus on the external through the teaching of behavior modification, the belief that people can change or modify behavior in and through their own strength and effort. Bookstores are loaded with books dealing with behavior modification when it comes to anger, negative thoughts, sexual immorality, etc. They all teach that change comes by finding ways to modify the behavior, whether through releasing tension (anger), teaching ourselves to have more positive thoughts (negative thoughts), learning self-control (sexual immorality), etc.

The same could be said about other religions as well. Both behavior modification and other world religions have a works-based morality and view of salvation. They both propose that with some clever thinking and self-determination, people can change whatever it is about them that is not good, or that they can earn favor from God. However, true and lasting change, internal and external, only comes by a heart transformed by the work of Jesus Christ.

What are some ways our culture tries to influence change in behavior without turning to the heart (Elf on the shelf, etc.)?

In what ways does an emphasis on a heart change go against a works-based view of religion?

THE AFTERLIFE

What comes to mind when you think of eternal life? Heaven? Streets of Gold? Well, Jesus helps us have a clear understanding of eternal life when he says, "This is eternal life: that they may know You, the only true God, and the One You have sent— Jesus Christ" (John 17:3). Sure, we can say that we will be with God in heaven one day, but that isn't the essence of eternal life. Eternal life is knowing Christ, communing with Him, and enjoying an ongoing relationship with Him. He is eternal life itself!

The unfortunate thing is that there are too many people who consider Jesus to be merely the ticket that is used to get to a blissful eternal life. They see Him as giving them access, and because of that access they get to avoid the eternal punishment of Hell. While there is truth to this, it also misses the mark in a significant way. Yes, Jesus does rescue the sinner from paying for his own sin in Hell, but He is also infinitely more than a ticket—He is eternal life. Jesus illustrates this point with one of His parables. In Matthew 13:44 Jesus says, "The kingdom of heaven is like treasure, buried in a field, that a man found and reburied. Then in his joy he goes and sells everything he has and buys that field." This is the way we are to see Jesus. We are to see Him as treasure, not as ticket. You don't treasure a ticket—you throw it away. But not with a treasure, and not with Jesus!

After hearing John 17:3, does this change your perspective on eternal life? If so, how?

How would you explain eternal life to someone now that you have this new perspective?

Discuss how it belittles Christ when we reduce Him to being a mere ticket who gives us access to heaven.

A NEW ANALOGY

I once heard a better analogy of world religions by comparing them to a maze instead of a mountain with various paths. Unlike the mountain where there are many paths that reach the top, with a maze, you only have one path that gets you to the center. Sure, there are other paths throughout the maze, but these paths only lead to dead ends. And like a maze, you often have paths that run parallel to each other for any given length of time, which is akin to the fact that there may be certain points of commonality between differing religions like the sanctity of human life, the existence of an afterlife, etc., even though these parallel paths eventually diverge. There is only one true path, one that makes it pass all of the dead ends and finally emerges as the sole way of truth to the center. And in a completely non-arrogant way, we have all reason and evidence to believe that true way is found in Christ Himself, who is "the way, the truth, and the life" (John 14:6).

Pluralistic beliefs like these have made religions look like a buffet line where we can just pick and choose a little of this and a little of that. I may take some Christian ethics, but I also want some Buddhism on the side, and maybe even a little pantheistic beliefs because, as we all know, the movie Avatar was really cool.

The analogy that the pluralist uses about the six blind men and the elephant doesn't accurately describe our situation. While the men might be blind, we are not. There is another observer, a seventh man that isn't blind, who sees plain as day that all of these blind observations are clearly that—blind! He sees what they fail to see, that what is really behind their sense of touch is merely that of an elephant.

The Christian worldview is much like this—we have an objective advantage, a birds-eye-view of things, not because of our own doing, but because God has revealed Himself to us through the pages of Scripture and through His Son, Jesus Christ. If God chose not to reveal Himself to us, then we would be left in the dark with many things. We would only be able to know general truths about Him, such as His power and goodness from our own observations of the things He has made. However, because He has spoken, because He has stooped down to our level to make Himself known, we can speak with confidence about those things concerning Himself.

WRAP UP

Remind students of the opening scenario we discussed at the start of this session. Invite them to revisit their initial answers and consider whether or not they would respond differently as a result of this discussion.

Take a few minutes to allow students to summarize some of the biggest personal "takeaways" from the session. For a helpful summary and main ideas, see page 62.

Discuss responses to the True Story. Invite students to consider how a similar experience might play out in their own lives.

Encourage students to complete the devotions for Session 4.

Finally, close with prayer, asking God for opportunities to lovingly share the truth of the gospel with those who don't know Jesus.

TRUE STORY

I got a part-time job working at the local mall during my senior year of high school. Near the kiosk where I worked in was another small kiosk owned and operated by two brothers. Not too long after moving in I introduced myself to them. We often chatted on account that the mall could be pretty slow moving at times. After a while, the topic of religion came up in our conversations. I learned that they were both Muslim, and they learned that I was a Christian. From then on, the topic of religion came up pretty frequently.

The conversations we had over our religious beliefs were cordial. I asked one of the brothers a lot of questions regarding his beliefs and why he believed them, and he was able to do the same for me. I learned early on that although he is a Muslim, he didn't believe himself to be a very good one. He admitted to not being committed or following through with the Five Pillars of Islam, especially when it came to prayer, fasting, and making the pilgrimage to Mecca. Because of his lack of works in these areas, he admitted to not having assurance of what awaited him in the afterlife.

Over the course of my time there I had many conversations with him, discussing topics like who Jesus is, how we are made right with God, whether salvation can be earned, as well as the credibility of the Bible versus that of the Koran. I was still young in my own faith at the time and maybe didn't have all the answers he needed to hear, but just engaging in the conversations allowed me to be strengthened in my own beliefs and grow in my ability to communicate those beliefs to others.

START

As you prepare to lead this session, read through the following content ahead of time, highlighting any information you would like to focus on during the group time. Note that italicized content on these pages is not part of the student material but is specific to your role in helping facilitate group discussion.

To begin the session, lead students through the following scenario. Keep in mind that it is not necessary to identify right or wrong answers. The purpose is to get students thinking and discussing potential answers to common apologetic questions. We will revisit this scenario toward the close of the session.

SET THE SCENE

It's a typical weekday morning when you hear the news reports that another massive terrorist attack has taken place in our country. The details from the media begin to pour in as reporters recount the dozens of innocent victims that have tragically lost their lives to the senseless acts of extreme violence. Men, women, and children all brutally gunned down, the innocent targets of people wanting to commit acts of evil and cause suffering. In one of the reports, you hear an interviewee, overcome by the horrific evil of these acts, ask, "If God exists, why did he allow this to take place? Why didn't he intervene?" The question resonates with you, and you begin to think how you would respond. What would you say to that person?

WATCH

≫

Direct students to use the video guide to follow along with the interview between Andy and William Lane Craig. Encourage them to fill in the blanks of the key statements, as well as write down additional notes on other important information in the space provided. Be sure to preview the session video ahead of time so you can develop your own notes to discuss during the group time.

FROM THE INTERVIEW:

For most people, suffering and evil is not an <u>intellectual</u> problem.

For most people, suffering and evil is an <u>emotional</u> problem.

Suffering is used by God to help bring people freely to a <u>knowledge</u> of Himself and to eternal life.

The <u>atheist</u> can't really say that there is evil in the world.

If anyone could complain of the problem of innocent suffering, it would be <u>Jesus</u> of <u>Nazareth</u>.

DISCUSS

Lead students through the following questions. As you walk students through this element of the session, highlight content you want to focus on. Select students to read aloud the Scripture passages, and invite them to share any additional questions or comments. .

What are your initial thoughts about the interview for this session?

What are some instances of evil and suffering that you have witnessed (or even personally experienced)?

Have you ever struggled with belief in God because of the existence of evil and suffering? If so, explain why.

Atheists try to use the existence of pain, evil, and suffering as an argument to prove God doesn't exist. Do you think that is possible? Explain. *If there are good reasons why God would permit evil and suffering to exist, then there is no contradiction.*

Why is it that atheists, who reject God, have no reason to believe in the existence of objective evil? How does their rejection of God actually hurt their argument? *If you do away with God, then you do away with objective goodness; and if you do away with objective goodness, you do away with its opposite—evil. By rejecting God, the atheist has no leg to stand on when trying to make moral pronouncements such as how human trafficking is wrong or racism is bad.*

Why is it important to make the distinction between the intellectual problem of evil and the emotional problem of evil?

Why is the existence of God and the existence of evil not logically incompatible?

What might be some good reasons for God to allow evil and suffering to take place in our world?

 WHY IS THERE EVIL AND SUFFERING IN THE WORLD?   **117**

When it comes to answering questions related to the topic of evil and suffering, it's important to recognize the true nature behind what's being asked. Consider the following examples:

» If God created a good world without sin, where did evil come from?

» Why did God allow my mom to die from cancer?

» Where was God during 9-11? Why didn't He stop the terrorists?

» If God loves me, why would I being going through so much pain over this broken relationship?

Which questions do you think are intellectual, emotional, or both?

What are some possible responses to questions like these?

DO WE SUFFER BECAUSE WE LACK FAITH?

There are some who would like us to believe that pain and suffering in our lives is the direct result of a lack of faith. "If only we had more faith," they claim, "would we experience the health, wealth, and prosperity in our lives that God desires."

Read Hebrews 11:1-34.

What is the common denominator shared between all of these heroes of the faith? *All of them lived "by faith."*

Were the things that happened to them because of their faith positive or negative? It is overwhelmingly positive, as seen in instances like crossing the Read Sea and the walls of Jericho falling, etc.

Read Hebrews 11:35-40.

What do the biblical heroes in these verses share in common with all of the others? *Again, they lived "by faith."*

Why is it important to emphasize that every person mentioned in this chapter lived by faith despite whether they suffered or not? It is important because this chapter completely overturned the idea that bad things happen to us when we lack faith. Every person in this chapter lived "by faith"—both those who escaped the edge of the sword as well as those who died by the sword.

Not only does Hebrews 11 dispel the myth that suffering comes from a lack of faith, but also consider the sufferings of the apostle Paul himself. In 2 Corinthians, Paul recounts some of his sufferings because of his faith and commitment to Christ when he says:

Five times I received 39 lashes from Jews. Three times I was beaten with rods by the Romans. Once I was stoned by my enemies. Three times I was shipwrecked. I have spent a night and a day in the open sea. On frequent journeys, I faced dangers from rivers, dangers from robbers, dangers from my own people, dangers from the Gentiles, dangers in the city, dangers in the open country, dangers on the sea, and dangers among false brothers; labor and hardship, many sleepless nights, hunger and thirst, often without food, cold, and lacking clothing.

Not to mention other things, there is the daily pressure on me: my care for all the churches (2 Cor. 11:24-28).

Why do you think Paul endured a life of such hardships?

What role do you think his faith played in being able to endure such sufferings?

The Bible doesn't promise an easy and carefree life to those who place their faith in Christ. In fact, Paul went so far as to say that "those who want to live a godly life in Christ Jesus will be persecuted" (2 Tim. 3:12). Persecution and suffering in this life is often the norm for those who have faith, for "the gate is wide and the road is broad that leads to destruction, and there are many who go through it. How narrow is the gate and difficult the road that leads to life, and few find it" (Matt. 7:13-14).

EVIL AND THE CROSS

In his book *No Easy Answers,* Dr. Craig tells the story of three men standing before God's throne on judgment day:

"Each had a score to settle with God. "I was hanged for a crime I didn't commit," complained one man bitterly. "I died from a disease that dragged on for months, leaving me broken in both body and spirit," said another. "My son was killed in the prime of his life when a drunk behind the wheel jumped the curb and ran him down," muttered the third. Each was angry and anxious to give God a piece of his mind. But when they reached the throne and saw their judge with His nail-scarred hands and feet and His wounded side, a "man of sorrows and acquainted with grief," each mouth was stopped."[1]

In other words, these men were silenced by the reality of the cross of Christ—the fact that Jesus, an innocent man, was abandoned by those closest to Him, arrested on trumped up charges, and unjustly sentenced to death in a way that is unimaginably brutal. His body, too, was broken, not only by the cross but also by lashings and beatings, and He, too, experienced inner conflict when the Father turned away as He bore our sins on the cross. Christ, who knew no sin, became sin on our behalf, so that in Him we might become the righteousness of God.

WRAP UP

Remind students of the opening scenario we discussed at the start of this session. Invite them to revisit their initial answers and consider whether or not they would respond differently as a result of this discussion.

Take a few minutes to allow students to summarize some of the biggest personal "takeaways" from the session. For a helpful summary and main ideas, see page 76.

Discuss responses to the True Story on the following page. Invite students to consider how a similar experience might play out in their own lives.

Before students leave, encourage them to complete the devotions for Session 5.

Close with prayer, asking God for His sustaining grace as we go through seasons of pain and suffering.

TRUE STORY

For the most part it was a typical Wednesday night youth gathering at the church. We were closing in on our walk-thru study of the Book of Genesis. I spoke. The praise band led worship. And there was plenty of time for socializing and fellowship among the student body.

At the end of our service, when everyone was preoccupied with either food or foosball, a student approached me with a serious look on her face. She had been visiting the church for a while by this point, coming with some friends who were committed members of the youth group. Having only spoken with her a few times, I wasn't quite sure what to expect. She began by talking about the lessons in Genesis we had recently covered, especially the ones regarding Joseph and how God had used the terrible things that had happened to him for his good in the end. I was encouraged by this news, especially since I was told by her friends in the group that she claimed to be agnostic in her beliefs about God.

The more she talked, the more I got the impression that she was holding something back. Given that most of her comments were about Joseph and the things he went through, I wondered if she might be wrestling with any particular pain or suffering in her own life. Without prying, I simply looked at her and said, "You know, I think we all know deep down that the world isn't the way it was supposed to be. And if that's the case, I wonder why we think that." Not knowing quite sure how that would land, I awaited her response. And from the tears welling up in her eyes, my suspicions were confirmed—she was struggling with the problem of evil in her world. After that, I was able to connect her with some godly women in our student ministry who would be able to go a little deeper into both the intellectual and emotional issues she was dealing with in response to the pain in her life.

Because everyone experiences suffering and the effects of evil on some level, having conversations over this topic can become a pretty frequent occurrence. Knowing what to say, and how to say it, is an invaluable tool in helping others navigate this big question that touches both the mind and the heart.

 WHY IS THERE EVIL AND SUFFERING IN THE WORLD?   **121**

START

≫

As you prepare to lead this session, read through the following content ahead of time, highlighting any information you would like to focus on during the group time. Note that italicized content on these pages is not part of the student material but is specific to your role in helping facilitate group discussion.

To begin the session, lead students through the following scenario. Keep in mind that it is not necessary to identify right or wrong answers. The purpose is to get students thinking and discussing potential answers to common apologetic questions. We will revisit this scenario toward the close of the session.

SET THE SCENE

You are enjoying a nice evening dinner with family at a local restaurant when the dinner conversation turns to the topic of what you plan to do after you graduate from high school. Almost instantly, questions begin to come from every direction, "Do you want to go to college?" "What do you want to study?" "What profession do you want to go into afterward?" Before you even get a chance to answer, a family member interjects by saying you should choose a major that leads to a high paying job. That's all that really matters. While the thought of being financially well-off is appealing, you wonder if choosing a profession for that reason alone is right. You wonder if there is more that goes into such a big decision. You consider whether your faith has anything to do with the matter. How do you respond?

WATCH

≫

Direct students to use the video guide to follow along with the interview between Andy and J. P. Moreland. Encourage them to fill in the blanks of the key statements, as well as write down additional notes on other important information in the space provided. Be sure to preview the session video ahead of time so you can develop your own notes to discuss during the group time.

FROM THE INTERVIEW

Apologetics is a <u>tool</u> to be used in the hands of every Christian in order to make much of Jesus.

Christians didn't think that learning to <u>think</u> well was part of being a <u>disciple</u>.

Apologetics gives a person a <u>confident</u>, settled faith.

You will not base your life on things you take to be <u>opinions</u>.

You will base your life on things you <u>know</u>.

You don't have to <u>know</u> all the answers.

DISCUSS

Lead students through the following questions. As you walk students through this element of the session, highlight content you want to focus on. Select students to read aloud the Scripture passages, and invite them to share any additional questions or comments. .

Read Matthew 22:37.

> He said to him, "Love the Lord your God with all your heart, with all your soul, and with all your mind."

Why do you think Jesus emphasized that we should love God with our minds?

Why is it important for Christians to not neglect loving God with their minds?

What does loving God with your mind look like? What are some ways you can strive to do better in this area?

Read Romans 12:1-2.

> Therefore, brothers, by the mercies of God, I urge you to present your bodies as a living sacrifice, holy and pleasing to God; this is your spiritual worship. Do not be conformed to this age, but be transformed by the renewing of your mind, so that you may discern what is the good, pleasing, and perfect will of God.

What is the connection between worship and having a transformed mind?

What are the benefits of having a renewed mind? *1) not being conformed to this world, and 2) being able to discern God's will.*

What does it mean to not be conformed to this world?

What does it mean to know the will of God?

How does one receive a renewed mind?

According to the apostle Paul, one aspect of worship involves the renewal of our minds. Once our minds are renewed and we allow the Word of God to saturate our minds and shape and mold our worldview, we can develop the ability to think biblically about other worldviews and beliefs that come our way.

 HOW CAN WE LIVE APOLOGETICALLY TODAY?   **123**

In addition, having a renewed mind helps us to live rightly before God (not being conformed to this world). In other words, it's not just about thinking rightly, but living rightly as well. This last point is important because sometimes our beliefs and actions don't line up. There are times that we say we believe something, but in fact we live very opposite of what we say we believe. Think about it this way:

STATED BELIEF +/- ACTUAL PRACTICE = ACTUAL BELIEF

Example:

» *Stated belief:* stealing is wrong

» *Actual practice:* copy a friend's homework assignment to avoid a grade penalty

» *Actual belief:* stealing is permissible in certain circumstances

Have you ever heard of Eleanor Boyer? Probably not, and that's okay. I don't imagine she'd want people knowing her name anyhow. Ms. Boyer, age 72 at the time, made the headlines several years ago on account that she won the New Jersey lottery of $11.8 million dollars (about $8 million after taxes).

What would you do if you won $8 million dollars? What do you think Ms. Boyer did?

If honest, most people would say they would keep a large portion of the winnings, perhaps giving some of it away to family and/or good causes that could benefit others. However, Ms. Boyer gave all of it away—every single dime—to places like her church, the local fire department, and other groups that served the town where she lived. "Why," you ask. In an article in *The New York Times*, Ms. Boyer stated that, "No new car, no vacation. My life is no different. I've given it up to God. I live in His presence and do His will, and I did that from the start."[1]

Ms. Boyer serves as a great example to living out our professed beliefs. She believed that God had always taken care of her, and that belief influenced every decision she made.

None of us live out something we are not convinced about. We look at the evidences, we hear the reasons, and after careful deliberation, we are all in. The same is true with life and apologetics. Apologetics helps us to see the reasons for why we believe what we believe, thus strengthening the faith and beliefs we have that then turn us toward a more consistent way of living.

CONVERSATIONAL APOLOGETICS

Remember that apologetics is a ministry to others as you seek to help remove any intellectual obstacles that may prevent someone from developing faith in Christ. It isn't about getting into arguments or winning debates; it is about making much of Jesus as we lovingly and graciously present Him to those around us.

Perhaps one of the best ways to begin practicing apologetics is by simply allowing it to seep into to everyday conversations. Look for opportunities to steer conversations, inviting (but not pressuring) people to explain why they believe what they believe, as well as opportunities to present your own reasons for the beliefs you have. If someone were to say in passing, "I can't believe people today are wanting to defund abortion groups," you could easily guide the conversation with a simple question like, "Why do you think that?" or "What led you to the conclusion that abortion is okay?"

Keep in mind that during conversations with others, you have a limited window of opportunity to speak up and ask questions—so be ready. Look for opportunities to learn more about the beliefs of the person you are speaking with. And when the time comes for you to present your own, be sure to keep in mind both what you say and how you say it—your tone is just as important as you words.

Always make it your goal to help people think through what they believe and why, and in turn allow yourself the opportunity to present why you believe what you believe as a Christian. By giving them the chance to speak, not only are you given credibility as a person who actually cares about them, but you are able to be in a better position of helping that person see any inconsistencies within their beliefs. Don't be overwhelmed with wondering whether you are going to say the wrong thing. Remain humble and kind to those you speak with. And take heart and gain confidence in knowing that the Christian worldview isn't the product of human invention, but is the revelation of God Himself.

Practicing apologetics can be difficult work, but that shouldn't come as a surprise. In essence, we are challenging people to think about their core beliefs, and at times, graciously telling them that they should abandon their worldview for the Christian worldview. That can be a lot for a person to take in. They have been living in their worldview for quite some time. Like a house they have lived in for decades, where they know every square inch and where everything has its place, we are suggesting that they relocate to a house and neighborhood to which they have no knowledge. Nobody likes to move and be uprooted from everything that is familiar to them, which is why the supernatural work of God in the hearts of people is necessary for genuine transformation to take place.

WRAP UP

Remind students of the opening scenario we discussed at the start of this session. Invite them to revisit their initial answers and consider whether or not they would respond differently as a result of this discussion.

Take a few minutes to allow students to summarize some of the biggest personal "takeaways" from the session. For a helpful summary and main ideas, see page 90.

Discuss responses to the True Story on the following page. Invite students to consider how a similar experience might play out in their own lives.

Encourage students to complete the devotions for Session 6.

Finally, close in prayer, asking God for grace as you and your students seek to love God with all of your minds.

TRUE STORY

When I was in graduate school years ago, I worked at a fitness club just down the road from where I lived. During my time there I became friends with an older gentleman named Henry. Henry would come to the gym every day around the same time. We would frequently talk while he was exercising, and through those natural conversations I got to know Henry pretty well. Over time I learned a lot of general things about him—where he was from, his family life, and so forth—and personal beliefs as well, such as his beliefs about God, life after death, and salvation. Uncovering what Henry believed about these things was never awkward. We were just two people who respected each other simply having a conversation.

It was through these simple conversations with a friend that I was able to present my own beliefs, the reasons I held them, and why he should consider them as alternatives to his own. For instance, Henry wasn't a Christian. He held to a pluralism of sorts (all religions are valid), so I was able to present the reasons why what he believed was not only logically contradictory, but how it also ignored the evidence and where the evidence leads. Not only that, but I was also able to get him to think differently about his own view of moral relativism, and how objective morality points to a single, objective Lawgiver (God).

I had many of these conversations with Henry over the course of several years, and during several I was able to present the gospel to him without any sense of awkwardness on either end. While it was always my intention to remove any intellectual obstacles to faith that Henry had, it never felt superficial given that our conversations were based on genuine friendship. Of course, that isn't to say that having cold-turkey conversations on personal religious beliefs isn't helpful—they certainly can be if done the right way. However, for me and many other apologists I know, the easiest and perhaps most effective way is to do apologetics in the context of having conversations with people, especially those with whom the Lord has already put in your path.

So get started with those around you. Have those conversations. Ask the right questions. Be on mission with Jesus as you give a defense for why you believe what you believe.

SOURCES

SESSION ONE

1. McGrath, *The Passionate Intellect* (InterVarsity Press: Downers Grove, IL., 2010), 19.

SESSION TWO

1. Peter Kreeft, *Fundamentals in the Faith: Essays in Christian Apologetics* (San Francisco: Ignatius, 1988), 25.

2. "Hitchens vs. Turek," Debate at Virginia Commonwealth University (8 Sept. 2008).

3. Thomas V. Morris, *Making Sense of It All* (Eerdmans:Grand Rapids, Mich., 1992), 61.

4. Ibid., p. 62.

5. C.S. Lewis, *The Weight of Glory* (HarperOne; HarperCollins REV ed., 2001.)

6. Augustine, *Confessions, 1.i.1*

SESSION THREE

1. Stephen Jay Gould, *Darwin's Revolution in Thought: An Illustrated Lecture for the Classroom* (2013).

2. Alister McGrath, *Mere Apologetics* (Baker Books: Grand Rapids, Mich., 2012), 101.

3. John Lennox, *God's Undertaker* (Lion Hudson: Oxford, England, 2007), 69.

4. Charles Darwin, *The Origin of Species* (Anniversary Edition; Signet, 2003).

SESSION FOUR

1. "Refugee Figures," UNHCR United Nations High Commisioner for Refugees [cited 14 March 2016]. Available from the Internet: *www.unhcr.org.*

SESSION FIVE

1. William Lane Craig, *No Easy Answers: Finding Hope in Doubt, Failure and Unanswered Prayer* (Chicago: Moody Press, 1990), p. 102.

2. C.S. Lewis, *The Problem of Pain* (HarperOne; Revised ed. 2015).

SESSION SIX

1. Andy Newman, "Lottery Winner Is Giving Her Millions Away," *The New York Times* [online], 10 Nov. 1997 [cited 18 March 2016]. Available from the Internet: *www.nytimes.com.*

Get the most from your study.

Customize your Bible study time with a guided experience and additional resources.

Big Questions: Developing a Christ-Centered Apologetic is a six-session apologetic study designed to equip students to think biblically and apologetically about some of today's toughest topics relating to the Christian faith. Bringing in some of today's leading Christian apologists to contribute—William Lane Craig, J.P. Moreland, Sean McDowell, and Craig Hazen— *Big Questions* takes students to another level of being able to explain why they believe what they believe. Questions relating to doubts, evidence for God's existence, the relationship between science and Christianity, the existence of world religions, the problem of evil and suffering, and how to live apologetically in the world today are covered throughout the study, all for the purpose of not only strengthening a student's faith, but to help that student defend and commend the faith to others.

Lifeway designs trustworthy experiences that fuel ministry. Today, the ministries of Lifeway reach more than 160 countries around the globe. For specific information on Lifeway Students, visit lifeway.com/students.